SAT/PSAT
WORD GAMES

Related Titles

501 Grammar and Writing Questions
501 Reading Comprehension Questions
Grammar Success in 20 Minutes a Day
Reading Comprehension Success in 20 Minutes a Day
Vocabulary and Spelling Success in 20 Minutes a Day
Write Better Essays in 20 Minutes a Day
Writing Skills Success in 20 Minutes a Day

SAT/PSAT WORD GAMES

Michele R. Wells

NEW YORK

Library of Congress Cataloging-in-Publication Data

Wells, Michele R.
  SAT/PSAT word games / Michele R. Wells. — 1st ed.
    p. cm.
  ISBN 978-1-57685-794-6
  1. Word games. 2. SAT (Educational test) 3. PSAT (Educational test)
I. Title.
  GV1507.W8W36 2011
  793.734--dc22
                              2010053647

Printed in the United States of America

9 8 7 6 5 4 3 2 1

First Edition

ISBN 978-1-57685-794-6

For more information or to place an order, contact LearningExpress at:
    2 Rector Street
    26th Floor
    New York, NY 10006

Or visit us at:
    www.learnatest.com

About the Author ▶

Michele R. Wells has been a writer and editor of test prep materials for companies such as The Princeton Review and Learning Express, LLC, since 2001. She volunteers regularly with the Everybody WINS Power Lunch program, a NYC-based literacy program for kids. A senior editor at one of the world's largest publishing companies, she has more than a decade of experience in nonfiction book and multimedia publishing. Michele holds a BA in dramatic writing and art history and is pursuing a master's in film, both from New York University.

About the Author

Acknowledgements

Jennifer Pollock, editor extraordinaire, conceptualized the idea for this book. Sheryl Posnick not only edited, but also dealt with various obstacles to make sure that this book came together as it should. Eric Titner, production editor, worked to make this book the best it could be. Thanks so much to all of you!

It's one thing to write about it, but Lauren Casteline King and Andrea Laurencell are in the trenches, teaching vocabulary and test preparation to students every day. A big thank you to both of you for taking the time to review the manuscript and provide feedback and advice.

And finally, writing two books in six months takes up a lot of time. Thanks to my family (Rita Sr., Rita Jr., Cheryl, John, Nathan, Colby, and Blake) for understanding where my priorities had to be this year.

Acknowledgements

Table of Contents ▶

PART III: Set a Foolproof Strategy

Introduction ▶

If you've picked up this book, you're probably interested in increasing your PSAT or SAT score. That means you're already aware of the effect these exams can have on your future, and that's great. But you've also got algebra homework to do, football games to attend, musical instruments and Spanish verbs to practice, chores to do, maybe an after-school job and other responsibilities, and—oh yeah—a social life to maintain. You don't have time to spend on more stuff related to school, much less exams that are probably months away at this point, right?

But think about it like this—you probably play games of some kind or another, either on your mobile phone, computer, or a game console, several times a week—maybe even every day. Playing those games can increase your online ranking, and maybe even make your friends jealous when you beat out their high scores, but playing the ones in this book can have a positive effect on your future. They can help you build a killer vocabulary and put yourself on stronger ground for gaining admission to the college of your choice.

Before we get to just how these games can help increase your scores, let's take a look at the test itself so you'll know exactly what to expect.

What Are the PSAT and SAT Exams?

The SAT is one of the two main standardized tests used by admissions teams to help evaluate your potential fit as a student at their colleges or universities. The SAT is designed to measure the verbal and mathematical skills you will need as you progress through your academic career. (The other main test is the ACT, which is designed to measure what you've learned in various academic subjects.)

The PSAT is an exam that not only prepares you to take the SAT, but also offers a chance to win National Merit Scholarships and access college- and career-planning tools through the College Board. The PSAT measures critical reading, writing, and math skills.

What Is the SAT Used For?

College admissions teams use your SAT score as part of the evaluation process, to decide if you will be a good addition to the diverse group of students at their schools. But that's not the only thing they look at—and frequently, it's not even the deciding factor.

Admissions teams look at individuals, not just scores and grades. They want well-rounded students, not just those who can churn out perfect tests or straight As.

Are you an athlete? Maybe you're an actor or a dancer? How about an artist? Do you do volunteer work, speak another language, or organize events for your school? Make sure you mention all these things on your application, because admissions teams are looking for students who can contribute to the diversity of campus life. So don't worry if your GPA isn't perfect—just be sure to highlight the great work you do in other areas of your life.

What Skills Are Tested on the SAT?

The SAT exam tests the skills you're currently learning in high school, and those which you'll need to do well in college: critical reading, writing, and mathematics. The critical reading section tests your knowledge of sentence completion and your ability to respond to reading passages. The writing section contains a short essay, as well as multiple-choice questions on grammar, usage, and error identification. The mathematics section tests your knowledge of algebra, geometry, statistics, arithmetic operations, and probability.

Who Takes the PSAT and SAT?

According to the College Board, the organization that administers the SAT, approximately two million students take the SAT every year. But here's a little secret—not all of them prepare for the exam in advance. By using this book, you're giving yourself an edge over the competition!

Where Do I Sign Up for the SAT?

Registration forms and information for the PSAT and SAT exams can be found at your school's guidance office, or you can register online at www.collegeboard.com. This website also offers detailed information about test dates in your area, practice tests, college-search and career information, information on sending your scores to the colleges of your choice, and many other services.

When Do I Take the SAT?

The SAT exam is offered several times a year, on Saturday mornings. You can find a schedule online at www.collegeboard.com, or at your school's guidance office. There is no limit to the number of times you can register for and take the exam.

If you're a high school freshman, don't worry about registering for the SAT yet—you've got plenty of time before you really need to take it. Although it couldn't hurt to start reading SAT prep books, working on your vocabulary, or doing other positive things (such as playing the games in this book!), your best bet at this point would be to focus on your studies and the extracurricular and civic activities that interest you.

Sophomores might consider taking the PSAT. The PSAT is usually taken in October, so make sure you use some of that free time you have in the summer to brush up, as National Merit Scholarships are awarded based on PSAT scores. If you are enrolled in any AP classes this year, you might also want to think about taking the corresponding SAT subject test as soon as you complete that course, so the information is still fresh in your mind.

If you're a high school junior or senior, you can take the SAT several times, up until December of your senior year. If you're planning to apply for early decision to any colleges or universities, you will need to prepare in the summer and take the SAT during or before October of your senior year.

Where Do I Take the SAT?

You can take the SAT on many high school and college campuses. When you register, you'll be given a list of sites in your local area; just pick the one that is most comfortable and convenient for you.

It's also a good idea to do a "dry run" before the actual test date— figure out how you'll get to the test site around the same time of day as your test (typically early in the morning), so you don't wind up getting surprised by road closures, construction, train or bus delays, bad online directions, or other things that can make you late (and stress you out!) on the day of the test.

How is the SAT Scored?

Okay, you did it—you've taken the SAT. Now what? The first thing that happens is that your answers are calculated into a score by computer. The points are awarded this way: For the Critical Reading and Math sections, one point is added for each correct answer and 1/4 point is subtracted for each incorrect multiple-choice answer. Nothing is subtracted for incorrect responses in the Math section or for questions you didn't answer.

Essays are scored by two independent readers (usually experienced high school or college teachers), who rate your work on a scale from 1 to 6. These scores are added together to produce a combined subscore. For example, if the first reader gives your essay a 5 and the second reader gives you a 6, your combined subscore would be an 11 (5 + 6). If you do not write an essay, you will receive a score of 0 on this section.

There is also an unscored section, which could be in the Critical Reading, Math, or multiple-choice Writing section. This section helps the College Board analyze whether the test is a fair and accurate representation of skills tested by the exam. Questions in the unscored section are not factored into your final SAT score.

Once your raw scores have been determined, they are then converted into a scaled score (from 200 to 800 for each test section, with additional subscores reported for the essay and multiple-choice writing questions).

How is Your Score Reported?

The College Board will send your scores to you. They will also send your scores to the schools you requested on your application. You can also send score reports to schools from your "My SAT" account on www.collegeboard.com, but you may have to pay a fee if you choose to send score reports after you've taken the exam.

How Did My Score Rate?

As of this writing, the average total score is around 1538, which breaks down to approximately 520 in Math, 510 in Writing, and 508 in Critical Reading. This average score is acceptable for most colleges and universities. Some schools require a score of 2100 or more, which would put you in the 90th percentile—meaning that you scored better than 90 percent of other test-takers during that particular exam.

A perfect score is 2400. Typically, fewer than 1 percent of all students who take the SAT get a perfect score.

What's the Deal with Percentile?

Your score report will also include two percentile rankings. The first measures your SAT exam scores against those of all students who took the test, nationwide. The second measures your scores against only the students in your state who took the test.

The higher your percentile ranking, the better. For example, if you receive a 65 in the national category and a 67 in the state category, that means your scores were better than 65 percent of students nationwide and 67 percent in your state. In other words, out of every 100 students who took the test in your state, you scored higher than 67 of them.

What If I Didn't Get the Score I Wanted?

Did you know that you can hide your lowest SAT scores? It used to be that students who didn't do as well as they would have liked on the SAT were stuck—the College Board sent all scores, even the embarrassing ones, to the colleges and universities to which the students had applied. But the College Board changed the rules recently, and now you're free to decide which scores you want them to send to prospective colleges. So, if you're not happy with your score, sign up to take the test again—and select the best combined score to be sent in with your application.

Now that you know what the tests are, how they are used, and what to expect on Test Day, let's get down to what you really want to know—how to use this book to get great results on the PSAT and SAT exams.

How to Use This Book

Preparing for the PSAT and SAT exams doesn't have to be a chore. Studies have shown that playing word games are an effective way to build your vocabulary—and even better, you'll have fun while you do it!

This book is broken into three sections:

In Part I, you'll learn how to break down difficult or unfamiliar words into easy-to-understand parts, and how to apply that knowledge to guess the meaning of these words. Part I also includes some general test-taking strategies.

Part II is the fun part—the games. In this section, you will work toward building an awesome vocabulary by doing crossword puzzles, word scrambles, acrostics, and more. The answers are provided at the end of each chapter, but try not to look at them unless you're absolutely, positively stumped. The games in this book are structured to help you work with spelling, learn new words, and improve your grammar. The games are made up of over 500 of the words most frequently found on the PSAT and SAT exams—so you can be confident that many of the words you're learning will turn up on test day.

The final section of this book contains test-taking strategies, checklists to help you prepare for the big day, and anxiety-busting exercises—to help ensure that you are at the top of your game when you walk into the testing facility to take the exam.

In the back of the book, you will find a glossary that defines all of the words used in this book, as well as a section on great books and websites you should check out for additional PSAT and SAT vocabulary word study.

Are you ready? Okay then—let's get started!

UNDERSTAND BASIC VOCABULARY SECRETS

1 ▶ Know Your Common Prefixes and Suffixes

Knowing the meaning of common prefixes and suffixes will help you figure out the definition of many familiar and unfamiliar words on the PSAT and SAT exams.

What Exactly Are Prefixes and Suffixes?

Prefixes and suffixes are attached to base words in order to add information and meaning. A **prefix** is an attachment that comes *before* a base word or stem. A **suffix** is an attachment that comes *after* the base word or stem. A **stem** is the main part of a word—the part that prefixes or suffixes are attached to—but might not actually be a full word by itself.

The word *repayment*, for example, is made up of the prefix *re-* (which means *again*), the stem *pay*, and the suffix *-ment* (which means *action* or *process*). So, with an understanding of suffixes, prefixes, and stems, you could figure out that the meaning of *repayment* is *the process of paying money back*.

Common Prefixes

The following are some examples of prefixes you might encounter when studying PSAT and SAT vocabulary words, along with their meanings.

a-, *ab-*, *an-* (apart or without)

ad- (toward or near)

ante- (before)

anti- (against)

auto- (self)

bi- (two)

bio- (life)

circum- (around)

co-, *com-*, *con-* (with or together)

de- (away or off)

di-, *dis-* (not or apart)

dys- (bad or problematic)

em-, *en-* (restrict or cause)

equi- (equal)

ex- (former)

extra-, *exo-* (outside of)

fore- (in front of or before)

hyper- (over)

hypo- (under)

geo- (earth)

im-, *in-* (not)

inter- (between)

micro- (tiny)

mis- (wrong)

mono- (one)

multi- (many)

neo- (new)

non- (not)

ob-, *oc-*, *of-*, *op-* (against, on, over, or toward)

omni- (all)

pan- (all)

para- (beyond)

peri- (around or about)

poly- (many)

post- (after)

pre- (before)

pro- (favoring or for)

re- (again)

retro- (backward)

semi- (half)

sub- (under or below)

super- (exceeding or above)

therm-, *thermo-* (heat)

trans- (across)

tri- (three)

un- (not)

Common Suffixes

-able, *-ible* (capable or worthy of)

-acy (state or quality)

-age (condition)

-al (act or process of, or pertaining to)

-ance, *-ence* (state or quality)

-ary (related to)

-ate (become)

-dom (place or state of being)

-en (make or become)

-er, *-or* (one who)

-esque (like or reminiscent of)

-gram, *-graph* (written or drawn)

-hood (class)

-*ic*, -*ical* (pertaining to)

-*iou*, -*ous* (characterized by)

-*ish* (having the quality of)

-*ive* (having the nature of)

-*less* (without)

-*log*, -*logue* (speech)

-*logy* (the study of)

-*oid* (resembles)

-*ory*, -*tory* (relating to)

-*ous* (possessing)

-*phile* (strong love for)

-*phobe*, -*phobia* (fear of)

-*ship* (position held)

-*y* (characterized by)

WORD DETECTIVE

Knowing prefixes and suffixes can help you deduce the meaning of many vocabulary words instantly, so familiarize yourself with the ones you don't already know for an instant vocab power-up!

Derivational Suffixes

There are suffixes that change the meaning of the base word or stem. These are called **derivational suffixes** (don't worry, you don't need to remember that), and some common examples are:

-*able*, -*ible* (capable of being)

-*ation*, -*sion*, -*tion* (state of being)

-*ful* (notable for)

-*fy* (make or become)

-*ify* (make or become)

-*ily* (in what manner)

-*ise*, -*ize* (become)

-*ism* (belief or doctrine)

-*ist* (one who)

-*ity*, -*ty* (having the quality of)

-*ment* (condition or result of)

-*ness* (state of being)

Derivational suffixes can combine with each other too, but the spelling may change (as in *predictability*, which is *predict* combined with -*able* and -*ity*).

Okay, now that you've reviewed some prefixes and suffixes and how they work, let's put that knowledge into action!

Exercise 1

Each word below contains a prefix. Using what you've learned, choose the best available definition.

1. microcosm
  a. to make something larger
  b. a sign of fear
  c. a smaller system which is representative of a larger one
  d. a vast expanse of land

2. foreshadow
  a. to darken
  b. to suggest something in advance
  c. to follow
  d. to retaliate

3. engender
  a. to bring into existence; to cause
  b. knowledge
  c. to promise to marry
  d. to grow

4. commingle
  a. to bring forward
  b. to mix or blend
  c. a quick movement
  d. to soften

5. extraordinary
  a. from the past
  b. exceptional or unusual
  c. from above
  d. large

Exercise 2

Each word below contains a suffix. Using what you've learned, choose the best available definition.

1. historical
   a. dry
   b. extremely funny
   c. something that belongs to a man
   d. relating to what happened in the past

2. provenance
   a. place or source of origin
   b. a gift
   c. the act of being proper or correct
   d. happiness

3. fiefdom
   a. a type of instrument
   b. unhappiness
   c. a domain controlled by a dominant person or lord
   d. a small area

4. travelogue
   a. a vacation
   b. a language
   c. confrontation
   d. the journal or documentation of a trip

5. humanoid
   a. resembling or having the characteristics of a human
   b. false or fake
   c. a very young person
   d. an alien

Exercise 3

Each word below contains a prefix and a suffix or derivational suffix. Using what you've learned, choose the best available definition.

1. decentralize
    a. to cause to be more populated
    b. in the very middle of an area
    c. to move downward
    d. to move away from an established main point

2. monograph
    a. a work of writing on a single subject
    b. a diverse group
    c. a drawing made with many colors
    d. a signature

3. apprehension
    a. to climb
    b. fearful expectation
    c. a course that comes before a meal
    d. the state of being angry

4. nullify
    a. to take apart
    b. to make invalid
    c. to bring together
    d. to make liquid

5. approbation
    a. a decision
    b. restriction
    c. concern
    d. official approval

Answers

Exercise 1

1. **c.** a smaller system which is representative of a larger one
2. **b.** to suggest something in advance
3. **a.** to bring into existence; to cause
4. **b.** to mix or blend
5. **b.** exceptional or unusual

Exercise 2

1. **d.** relating to what happened in the past
2. **a.** place or source of origin
3. **c.** domain controlled by a dominant person or lord
4. **d.** the journal or documentation of a trip
5. **a.** resembling or having the characteristics of a human

Exercise 3

1. **d.** move away from an established main point
2. **a.** work of writing on a single subject
3. **b.** fearful expectation
4. **b.** make invalid
5. **d.** official approval

2 ▶ Learn Root Words

Now that you know the meanings that prefixes and suffixes bring to vocabulary words, you're ready to review the most common *roots*—the base of the words to which prefixes and suffixes are attached. Once you know these, you can guess the meaning of almost any unfamiliar word on the PSAT and SAT exams.

Root Words

English is made up of words derived from Latin and Greek roots, as well as words from German, French, and other languages. Any familiarity you have with other languages can be an advantage when trying to guess the meaning of a word, because if you can recognize even a small part of it, you've improved your chances of figuring out the definition.

List of Common Root Words

acro (top, height, tip)

aer, aero (air)

aesth, esth (beauty)

agr, agri, agro (farm)

alg, algo (pain)

ambi, amphi (both)

ambul (move)

ami, amo (love)

andr, andro (male)

anim (spirit, life)

ann, enn (year)

anth, antho (flower)

anthrop, anthropo (human)

apo, apho (away, separate)

aqu, aqua (water)

arbor (tree)

arch (most important)

archa, archae, archi (ancient)

art (skill)

arthr, arthro (joint)

aster, astr (star)

act (to do)

audi (to hear)

avi (bird)

bar, baro (pressure)

bell, belli (war)

bene (good)

bibli (book)

bio (life)

blast (cell)

capt, cept (capture, hold)

cardi, cardio (heart)

carn, carni (flesh)

caust, caut (burn)

cede, ceed (yield)

ceive, cept (take)

celer (fast)

cent, centi (hundred)

centr, centro (center)

cephal, cephalo (head)

chrom, chromo, chromat, chromato (color)

cide, cise (cut)

circle, circum (around)

claim, clam (speak)

cline (lean)

cogn, cogni (learn)

cred (believe)

crypto (hidden)

cycl (circle)

dem, demo (people)

dendr, dendri, dendro (tree)

dent, dont (tooth)

derm, derma (skin)

dic, dict (speak)

domin (master)

don, donat (give)

duc, duct (lead)

dyn, dyna, dynam (power)

ego (self)

endo (inside)

equ, equi (equal)

fer (carry)

flect (bend)

flor, flora, fleur (flower)

fract, frag (break)

fug (escape)

gastr, gastro (stomach)

gen, gene, geno (birth)

geo (earth)

List of Common Root Words *(continued)*

ger (old age)

gram (written)

gyn (female)

helic, helico (spiral)

heli, helio (sun)

hem, hema, hemo (blood)

herbi (plant)

hetero (other)

homeo, homo (same)

hydr, hydro (water)

imag (likeness)

iso (equal)

ject (throw)

jud, jur, just (law)

junct (join)

juven (young)

kine, kinet (motion)

lab (work)

later (side)

liber (free)

lingu (language)

loc (place)

locu, loqu (speak)

log, logo (word)

luc, lumin (light)

lun, luna, lumi (moon)

mal, male (bad)

mand (order)

mania (madness)

manu (hand)

mar, mari (sea)

mater, matr, matri (mother)

meter (measure)

migr (move)

morph (form)

mort (death)

narr (tell)

nat (born)

necr, necro (dead)

neg (no)

nom, nomin (name)

noun, nunc (declare)

numer (number)

ocu, op, opt (eye)

op, oper (work)

ortho (straight)

pale, paleo (ancient)

pater, patr, patri (father)

path (feeling)

ped, pede, pedi, pod (foot, child)

phag, phage (eat)

phil (friend, love)

phon, phono (sound)

phot, photo (light)

phys (body, nature)

pop (people)

pseud, pseudo (false)

psych, psycho (mind)

pugn, pugna (fight)

purg (clean)

pyr, pyro (fire)

rid (laugh)

rupt (burst)

scend (climb)

sci (know)

scrib, script (write)

sect (cut)

serv (keep)

sol (alone, sun)

spec, spect, spic (see)

sphere (ball)

spir (breathe)

stell (star)

techno (skill)

tel, tele, telo (far)

tele (far away)

temp, tempo (time)

term, termin (end)

ter, terr, terra (earth)

the, theo (god)

therm, thermo (heat)

urb (city)

vac (empty)

verb (word)

vid, vis (to see)

WATCHING FOR WORDS

There's no way to provide a complete list of all root words that occur in the English language, but the list provided is a great start to figuring out many PSAT/SAT vocabulary word meanings. As you go through your daily life, keep an eye out for more word roots, and watch for them to reappear in other words. The more you know, the more you can figure out—and the better your vocabulary will be!

Now, let's try some exercises to put your knowledge of root word meanings to work.

Exercise 1

Using what you've learned, choose the best available definition for each word.

1. genuflect
 a. to run
 b. to bend at the knee
 c. to jump
 d. to solve

2. intercept
   a. to make known
   b. to come together
   c. to seize or hold before arrival
   d. to come between

3. concede
   a. to hinder
   b. to return
   c. to display arrogance
   d. to yield or accept as true

4. carnivorous
   a. looking for danger
   b. feeding on animal flesh
   c. seeking out parties or events
   d. excitable

5. inscription
   a. enrollment
   b. the beginning
   c. the writing or dedication on something
   d. a disaster

Exercise 2

Using what you've learned, fill in the correct letters to complete the word base.

1. An instrument used to measure the <u>pressure</u> of the atmosphere:

   __ __ __ __ meter

2. Marine animals that move by expelling water from a tube under

   the <u>head</u>: __ __ __ __ __ __ __ pod

3. Moving in a direction away from a <u>center</u> or axis:

__ __ __ __ __ ifugal

4. The study of the operation of <u>air</u>crafts: __ __ __ __ nautics

5. The act of <u>speaking</u> words that are to be written or transcribed:

__ __ __ __ ation

6. To make something move in a way that resembles <u>life</u>like action:

__ __ __ __ ate

7. Something done out of <u>love</u> for or goodwill toward others:

__ __ __ __ anthropy

8. To <u>cut</u> into: in __ __ __ __

9. The process of <u>learn</u>ing: __ __ __ __ ition

10. A particular concept or understanding of <u>beauty</u>:

__ __ __ __ __ etics

Answers

Exercise 1

1. **b**. to bend at the knee
2. **c**. to seize or hold before arrival
3. **d**. to yield or accept as true
4. **b**. feeding on animal flesh
5. **c**. the writing or dedication on something

Exercise 2

1. <u>b a r o</u> meter
2. <u>c e p h a l o</u> pod
3. <u>c e n t r</u> ifugal
4. <u>a e r o</u> nautics
5. <u>d i c t</u> ation
6. <u>a n i m</u> ate
7. <u>p h i l</u> anthropy
8. in <u>c i s e</u>
9. <u>c o g n</u> ition
10. <u>a e s t h</u> etics

3 ▶ Deconstruct and Rebuild

In Chapter 1, you learned the meanings of common prefixes and suffixes. In Chapter 2, you learned the meanings of common base words. Now, it's time to put this knowledge to use.

Let's practice before moving on to the more complex vocabulary needed to play the games in the next section of the book, and on the PSAT and SAT exams.

In the following exercises, put it all together by combining base words with prefixes and suffixes to create new words.

Exercise 1

Match the word parts from column A to the word parts in column B to create words that match the definitions that follow. Some word parts will be used more than once.

Column A	Column B
anti	act
con	cede
de	ceed
ex	ceive
in	cept
mis	dict
non	flect
pre	mand
re	serve
un	spect

1. To keep or store; protect: _____
2. To respond or change due to a stimulus: _____
3. To go over and above: _____
4. To charge with an offense: _____
5. To keep safe; to avoid wasteful use of: _____
6. To trick; to be false: _____
7. To order or send back; to return to custody: _____
8. An idea: _____
9. Special regard or esteem: _____
10. To foretell or declare in advance: _____
11. To cause to begin; to form: _____
12. A command or principle intended as a general course of action:

    _____
13. To be worthy of something: _____
14. To turn aside: _____
15. To acquire or come into possession: _____
16. To ask with authority: _____

17. With the exclusion of: _____

18. To view critically or closely: _____

19. To keep back or hold: _____

20. To surpass; to go ahead or in front of: _____

Exercise 2

Match the word parts from column A to the word parts in column B to create words that match the definitions that follow. Some will be used more than once. An asterisk (*) denotes that two entries from column B are used (don't forget to drop the silent *e* if necessary).

Column A	Column B
auto	ance
bio	ary
cardio	ate
jur	ation
kinet	ic
lumin	graph
migr	logy
narr	ous
opt	or
phon	y

1. An instrument that measures the movement of the heart: _____

2. Emitting or reflecting light: _____

3. The act of moving from one country or region to another: _____

*4. Of or relating to a signature: _____

5. One who is sworn to give a verdict in a dispute: _____

6. The study of living organisms: _____

7. To tell a story in detail: _____

8. Of or relating to the eye: _____

9. Of or relating to sound: _____

*10. The written story of someone's life: _____

.11. The study of the heart: _____

12. A body of people who are called on to give a verdict in a dispute: _____

13. Of or related to motion: _____

14. The state or quality of emitting or reflecting light: _____

*15. One who tells a story in detail: _____

16. A person of prominence or brilliance: _____

17. Not genuine; false: _____

18. A signature: _____

19. The act of telling or recounting a story in detail: _____

20. To move from one country or region to another: _____

Exercise 3

Insert definitions for the following words based on your knowledge of prefixes, suffixes, and base word meanings.

1. bibliomania: _____

2. enumerate: _____

3. vacuous: _____

4. temporal: _____

5. autobiographic: _____

6. paternally: _____

7. chromatograph: _____

8. bioavailability: _____

9. amphibious: _____

10. anthropologic: _____

Answers

Exercise 1

1. preserve
2. react
3. exceed
4. indict
5. conserve
6. deceive
7. remand
8. concept
9. respect
10. predict
11. conceive
12. precept
13. deserve
14. deflect
15. receive
16. demand
17. except
18. inspect
19. reserve
20. precede

Exercise 2

1. cardiograph
2. luminous
3. migration
*4. autographic
5. juror
6. biology
7. narrate
8. optic
9. phonic
*10. biography

11. cardiology
12. jury
13. kinetic
14. luminance
*15. narrator
16. luminary
17. phony
18. autograph
19. narration
20. migrate

Exercise 3

Answers will vary; possible answers are provided.

1. bibliomania: extreme love or passion for books
2. enumerate: to determine the number of
3. vacuous: emptied; lacking content
4. temporal: relating to time
5. autobiographic: about one's self
6. paternally: relating to a father
7. chromatograph: an instrument for analyzing color
8. bioavailability: the rate at which a substance is absorbed into an organism
9. amphibious: able to exist on land and in water
10. anthropologic: relating to the study of humans

Build an Awesome Vocabulary with Games

4 ▶ Crossword Puzzles

In this chapter, you'll put what you've learned in Part I to use with these fun vocabulary-building crossword puzzles.

Instructions

Using the clues that follow each puzzle, solve by filling in the white squares to form PSAT and SAT vocabulary words. The answers will read from left to right or from top to bottom.

If you need help, a word list containing all the words used in this chapter can be found on page 38. Scan the list to see if you can identify the word you're looking for. If you're completely stumped, give yourself a break by turning to another game or doing something else for a while. You can always come back and finish a game at another time.

Answers to all the puzzles can be found at the end of the chapter—but don't peek until you've given each game your very best shot!

Crossword Puzzle #1:
Spoken Word

The answers to this puzzle all have something to do with speaking or reciting. If you get stuck, take a look at the word list at the end of the chapter to see if you can find the word to match the definition in the clue.

Across
3. An overused expression.
6. Correct and proper inflection and intonation in speech.
7. Ranting speech.
12. A short story or account of something interesting.
13. Speaking two languages.
15. Quiet; not inclined to speak.
16. A statement that is widely accepted as true.
17. A statement of values.
19. To implore or beg.

Down
1. Blatant; conspicuous and offensive outcry.
2. To plead with or urge someone to action.
4. Vocabulary.
5. To make defamatory or contemptuous statements.
8. To give notice; tell.
9. Talkative.
10. Slang.
11. An official command or instruction.
12. To express well in words.
14. A phrase that cannot be translated literally into another language.
18. A negative or disparaging remark.

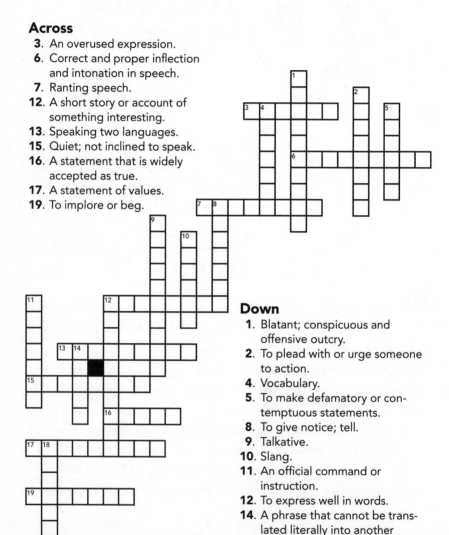

Crossword Puzzle #2:
War and Peace

The words in this puzzle can be used in the context of the military, battle, or warfare. If you get stuck, take a look at the word list at the end of the chapter to see if you can find the word to match the definition in the clue.

Across

3. To vanquish completely; make someone or something cease to exist.
4. To decode; interpret.
9. To free from the power or control of others; release from bondage.
10. Someone who lives by plundering or theft.
12. Someone who opposes war.
14. To give up a position of leadership.
15. Warlike.
17. To avoid or escape.
18. Treachery; betrayal.
20. A tactic; a deliberate, coordinated movement.

Down

1. To examine in detail; to seek orders or votes.
2. To put into danger; threaten.
5. Acting like a tyrant.
6. Suited for war; related to military life.
7. A police officer or soldier, especially in France.
8. To move to action; stir up.
11. To wipe out completely.
13. To seize by force.
16. To push out of a position of authority.
19. To destroy or reduce drastically.

Crossword Puzzle #3: Order in the Court

In this puzzle, all the words you'll find will have something to do with legal disputes or the courtroom. If you get stuck, take a look at the word list at the end of the chapter to see if you can find the word to match the definition in the clue.

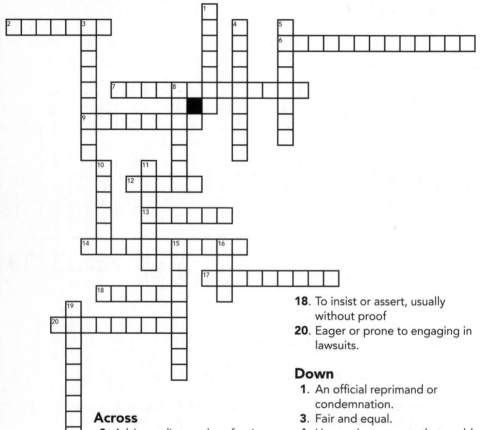

18. To insist or assert, usually without proof
20. Eager or prone to engaging in lawsuits.

Down

1. An official reprimand or condemnation.
3. Fair and equal.
4. Happenings; events that could lead to a grave consequence.
5. To argue in favor of something; a person who argues in favor of something.
8. A law or legislative act.
10. To agree.
11. To argue or debate; oppose; verbal disagreement or controversy.
15. Opponent.
16. Burden or responsibility.
19. Made less severe.

Across

2. Advice, policy, or plan of action.
6. Unbiased; fair.
7. The philosophy, science, and study of law.
9. To intimidate with strong language.
12. A written statement that is false and malicious.
13. To read carefully.
14. The resolution of a dispute by an impartial party.
17. Fair and equal; having good judgment or common sense.

Crossword Puzzle #4:
A Dark and Stormy Night

The answers in this puzzle can all be found in spooky stories. If you get stuck, take a look at the word list at the end of the chapter to see if you can find the word to match the definition in the clue.

Across

5. Able to perceive things (such as the future).

7. A prediction, omen, or sense of doom.

9. Obscure; requiring secret or mysterious knowledge.

11. A lyric poem lamenting the dead.

15. Dreary; barren.

18. Horrible or terrifying.

19. Of or relating to a burial or grave.

20. Of or related to the night.

Down

1. Wishing harm to others.

2. A ghost-like appearance.

3. Fearful.

4. Bloody; gory.

6. Suspicious; fearful.

8. A somber, mournful song, usually for the dead.

10. A city of the dead.

12. Harmful or evil.

13. Extremely wicked.

14. Foreshadowing evil; foreboding.

16. A person who foretells events or sees the future.

17. Hidden; mysterious.

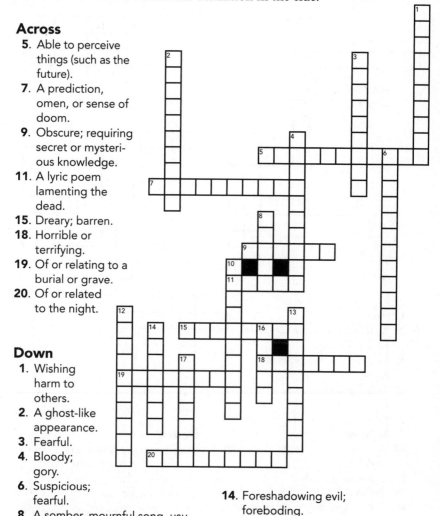

Crossword Puzzle #5: Love and Marriage

Words in this puzzle can all be used in the context of romance—love, marriage, infatuation, and everything in between. If you get stuck, take a look at the word list at the end of the chapter to see if you can find the word to match the definition in the clue.

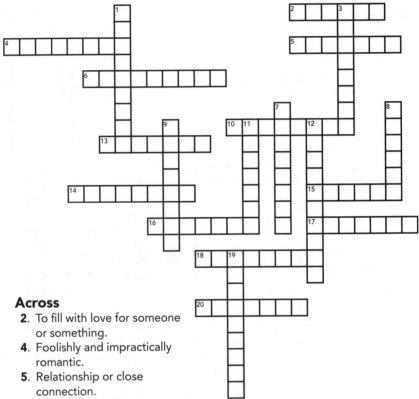

Across

2. To fill with love for someone or something.
4. Foolishly and impractically romantic.
5. Relationship or close connection.
6. Of or related to the relationship between spouses.
10. A relationship or special feeling of closeness.
13. Promise to marry.
14. Unlawful or illicit lover.
15. Passionate; giving off intense heat.
16. Harmony; mutual understanding.
17. Showing love.
18. Kiss.
20. Of or relating to marriage.

Down

1. To come to terms; bring back together; make compatible.
3. Hatred of marriage.
7. Loyalty; devotion.
8. A narrative poem, often in lyric form and about love.
9. Of or relating to marriage; matrimonial.
11. Hot; passionate.
12. Foolishly or extravagantly in love.
19. Cared for; loved.

Crossword Puzzle #6: An Apple a Day

You will often hear the answers in this puzzle in doctor's offices or hospitals. If you get stuck, take a look at the word list at the end of the chapter to see if you can find the word to match the definition in the clue.

Across

5. To make better; lessen the seriousness.
7. To waste away; cause to lose flesh.
12. A remedy for all diseases and ills.
13. Sterile; thoroughly clean and free of disease.
14. To lessen; make better.
15. Of or related to birth.
16. Occurring among members of a family.
17. To become fixed or rigid.
18. Of or related to the eye.
19. Swell out.
20. To introduce a microorganism in order to treat or prevent a disease; vaccinate.

Down

1. Of or related to the sense of smell.
2. Inbuilt; genetic.
3. To rouse; excite to activity.
4. Just begun; in early stages of development.
6. Deep or instinctive; relating to the innards.
8. Existing or present, but concealed or inactive.
9. To wither away; decay.
10. To vomit; to throw back exactly.
11. To examine closely.

Crossword Puzzle #7: The Natural World

This puzzle features words that all have to do with different facets of nature—plants, animals, farming, and growing. If you get stuck, take a look at the word list at the end of the chapter to see if you can find the word to match the definition in the clue.

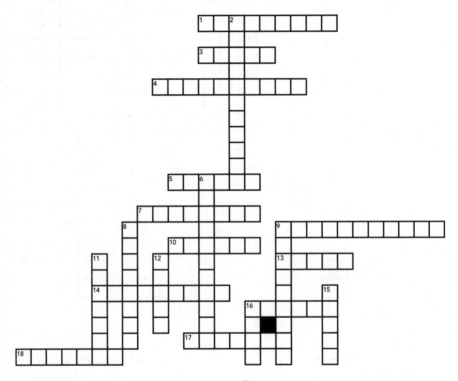

Across
1. Of or related to plants.
3. Able to withstand adverse conditions.
4. Occurring naturally or originating in a particular region.
5. Workable; able to grow.
7. Of or related to trees.
9. Feeding only on plants.
10. Fertile; fruitful.
13. Strong saline or salt water.
14. To nurture; prepare and improve.
16. Capable of growing crops.
17. Animal-like.
18. A young ox or steer.

Down
2. Of or relating to earth or land.
6. The science or practice of farming.
8. Young animal between one and two years of age.
9. Suitable for living.
11. Of or related to the countryside and farming.
12. Corn.
15. Wild; untamed.
16. Extremely dry; lacking sufficient rainfall.

Crossword Puzzle #8: Money Matters

The answers within this puzzle all relate to money and finance. If you get stuck, take a look at the word list at the end of the chapter to see if you can find the word to match the definition in the clue.

Across

2. A person who gives charitable gifts.
3. Begging for money or food.
6. Someone who would do anything for money.
9. Wasteful and extravagant behavior.
11. To lessen or reduce.
14. Insignificant; a small amount.
15. Habitually lacking money; poor.
17. Completely impoverished.
18. Stinginess.
19. To steal money by falsifying documents.
20. Property pledged as security for a debt; accompanying; secondary.

Down

1. Not generous; unwilling to spend.
4. Economical.
5. Miserly.
7. Wealthy, rich.
8. Extreme poverty; lack of essential necessities.
10. Fake.
12. A very small sum.
13. Generosity; giving or bestowing liberally.
16. Extreme poverty.

Crossword Puzzle #9: The Write Stuff

Words relating to the art and craft of writing make up the answers to this puzzle. If you get stuck, take a look at the word list at the end of the chapter to see if you can find the word to match the definition in the clue.

Across

6. Of or relating to letters and letter-writing.
8. Tell a story.
9. Ambiguous, indirect, and wordy language.
13. Unoriginal.
15. Concerned with writing and spelling.
16. Wordy.
17. Collection of writings.
18. A written history; to write a history.
19. Figurative; not literal.

Down

1. Writing materials; notepaper.
2. Complicated; long-winded.
3. To shorten or edit down, keeping the essential elements.
4. Brief or terse in writing or speech.
5. Overused; trite.
7. Of or along or relating to a line.
9. Forming a whole; sticking together.
10. Obsession with books.
11. To go off-subject; turn attention away.
12. Capable of being read or deciphered.
14. A large book.

Crossword Puzzle #10:
The Rainbow Connection

The answers to this puzzle pertain to different forms of art and artists. If you get stuck, take a look at the word list at the end of the chapter to see if you can find the word to match the definition in the clue.

16. A range or particular use of color; a flat tray to hold paint.
17. Dark-colored.

Across
1. To whiten; turn pale.
5. Having a reddish color.
6. A person who excels in an art (especially music).
8. Bright, beaming.
9. Someone who dabbles in the arts.
12. Without hue; free from color.
13. Furnace or oven for drying or hardening pottery or bricks.
14. Tightly woven material used for tents and sails; a framed cloth for painting.

Down
2. Red in color; furious.
3. Multicolored.
4. Appreciation of beauty or art.
5. Glowing.
7. Showing varying rainbow colors.
10. Glowing brightly; radiant.
11. A craftsperson.
12. A light shade of blue.
15. Green in color.
16. Pale; lacking color.

Word List for Chapter 4

abdicate	aspersion	chronicle	dispute
abridge	assuage	circumlocution	distend
achromatic	atrophy	clairvoyant	elegy
adversary	augur	cliché	elocution
advocate	axiom	cohesive	elude
aesthetic	azure	collateral	emaciate
affinity	ballad	concur	emancipate
affluent	bellicose	conjugal	embezzle
agriculture	benefactor	connubial	enamor
allege	beseech	convoluted	epistolary
amorous	bestial	counsel	equitable
anecdote	betroth	counterfeit	fecund
annihilate	bibliomania	cryptic	feral
anthology	bilingual	cultivate	fervent
antiseptic	blanch	curtail	fidelity
apparition	botanical	decimate	foreboding
apprehensive	brigand	decipher	frugal
apprise	brine	derivative	funereal
arable	browbeat	desolate	gendarme
arbitration	bucolic	despotic	ghastly
arboreal	bullock	destitute	habitable
arcane	canvas	digress	hackneyed
arid	canvass	dilettante	harangue
articulate	censure	dirge	hardy
artisan	cherished	dispassionate	herbivorous

hereditary	loquacious	ocular	reconcile
idiom	luminous	olfactory	regurgitate
impecunious	maize	ominous	resplendent
incidents	maleficent	onus	ruddy
incite	malevolent	orthographical	sanguinary
indigence	malign	osculate	scrutinize
indigenous	mandate	ossified	stationery
infatuated	maneuver	oust	statute
inherent	manifesto	pacifist	stimulate
inoculate	marital	palette	stingy
iridescent	martial	palliate	swarthy
jargon	mendicancy	pallid	taciturn
jeopardize	mercenary	panacea	terrestrial
judicious	metaphorical	paramour	tome
jurisprudence	misogamy	parsimony	torrid
kiln	mitigated	penurious	tremulous
kinship	munificent	perfidy	usurp
laconic	narrate	persuade	variegated
latent	nascent	peruse	verbose
legible	natal	pittance	verdant
lexicon	necropolis	privation	viable
libel	nefarious	profligacy	virtuoso
linear	nocturnal	quixotic	visceral
litigious	nominal	radiant	vociferous
livid	obliterate	rapport	yearling

Answers

Crossword Puzzle #1: Spoken Word

Across

3. cliché
6. elocution
7. harangue
12. anecdote
13. bilingual
15. taciturn
16. axiom
17. manifesto
19. beseech

Down

1. vociferous
2. persuade
4. lexicon
5. malign
8. apprise
9. loquacious
10. jargon
11. mandate
12. articulate
14. idiom
18. aspersion

Crossword Puzzle #2: War and Peace

Across

3. annihilate
4. decipher
9. emancipate
10. brigand
12. pacifist
14. abdicate
15. bellicose
17. elude
18. perfidy
20. maneuver

Down

1. canvass
2. jeopardize
5. despotic
6. martial
7. gendarme
8. incite
11. obliterate
13. usurp
16. oust
19. decimate

Crossword Puzzle #3: Order in the Court

Across
2. counsel
6. dispassionate
7. jurisprudence
9. browbeat
12. libel
13. peruse
14. arbitration
17. judicious
18. allege
20. litigious

Down
1. censure
3. equitable
4. incidents
5. advocate
8. statute
10. concur
11. dispute
15. adversary
16. onus
19. mitigated

Crossword Puzzle #4: A Dark and Stormy Night

Across
5. clairvoyant
7. foreboding
9. arcane
11. elegy
15. desolate
18. ghastly
19. funereal
20. nocturnal

Down
1. malevolent
2. apparition
3. tremulous
4. sanguinary
6. apprehensive
8. dirge
10. necropolis
12. maleficent
13. nefarious
14. ominous
16. augur
17. cryptic

Crossword Puzzle #5: Love and Marriage

Across

2. enamor
4. quixotic
5. kinship
6. connubial
10. affinity
13. betroth
14. paramour
15. torrid
16. rapport
17. amorous
18. osculate
20. marital

Down

1. reconcile
3. misogamy
7. fidelity
8. ballad
9. conjugal
11. fervent
12. infatuated
19. cherished

Crossword Puzzle #6: An Apple a Day

Across

5. palliate
7. emaciate
12. panacea
13. antiseptic
14. assuage
15. natal
16. hereditary
17. ossified
18. ocular
19. distend
20. inoculate

Down

1. olfactory
2. inherent
3. stimulate
4. nascent
6. visceral
8. latent
9. atrophy
10. regurgitate
11. scrutinize

Crossword Puzzle #7: The Natural World

Across

1. botanical
3. hardy
4. indigenous
5. viable
7. arboreal
9. herbivorous
10. fecund
13. brine
14. cultivate
16. arable
17. bestial
18. bullock

Down

2. terrestrial
6. agriculture
8. yearling
9. habitable
11. bucolic
12. maize
15. feral
16. arid

Crossword Puzzle #8: Money Matters

Across

2. benefactor
3. mendicancy
6. mercenary
9. profligacy
11. curtail
14. nominal
15. impecunious
17. destitute
18. parsimony
19. embezzle
20. collateral

Down

1. stingy
4. frugal
5. penurious
7. affluent
8. privation
10. counterfeit
12. pittance
13. munificent
16. indigence

Crossword Puzzle #9: The Write Stuff

Across
6. epistolary
8. narrate
9. circumlocution
13. derivative
15. orthographical
16. verbose
17. anthology
18. chronicle
19. metaphorical

Down
1. stationery
2. convoluted
3. abridge
4. laconic
5. hackneyed
7. linear
9. cohesive
10. bibliomania
11. digress
12. legible
14. tome

Crossword Puzzle #10: The Rainbow Connection

Across
1. blanch
5. ruddy
6. virtuoso
8. radiant
9. dilettante
12. achromatic
13. kiln
14. canvas
16. palette
17. swarthy

Down
2. livid
3. variegated
4. aesthetic
5. resplendent
7. iridescent
10. luminous
11. artisan
12. azure
15. verdant
16. pallid

5 ▶ Anagrams

In this chapter, you will deconstruct a PSAT/ SAT vocabulary word to find at least 10 new words hidden inside. If any of these vocabulary words are unfamiliar, be sure to look them up in the glossary at the back of the book.

Instructions

Rearrange the letters in each PSAT/SAT vocabulary word to spell as many new words as you can. Each word must be made up of a minimum of three letters—one- and two-letter words do not count. Try to find at least 10 words for each before moving on to the next puzzle.

For an extra challenge, set a timer or stopwatch for 10 minutes. See how many words you can find before time is up!

The answers are found at the end of the chapter. If you're not familiar with some of the words you find in the answer key, look them up in a dictionary to supercharge your word power!

Anagram Puzzle #1

PARAGON

_____

_____

_____

_____

_____

_____

_____

_____

_____

Anagram Puzzle #2

ARDUOUS

_____

_____

_____

_____

_____

_____

_____

_____

_____

Anagram Puzzle #3

DISDAIN

_____

_____

_____

_____

_____

_____

_____

_____

_____

_____

Anagram Puzzle #4

WISTFUL

_____

_____

_____

_____

_____

_____

_____

_____

_____

_____

Anagram Puzzle #5

VARIED

_____

_____

_____

_____

_____

_____

_____

_____

_____

Anagram Puzzle #6

TIRADE

_____

_____

_____

_____

_____

_____

_____

_____

_____

Anagram Puzzle #7

BEDLAM

_____

_____

_____

_____

_____

_____

_____

_____

_____

Anagram Puzzle #8

CALLOUS

_____

_____

_____

_____

_____

_____

_____

_____

_____

Anagram Puzzle #9

RIBALD

_____

_____

_____

_____

_____

_____

_____

_____

_____

Anagram Puzzle #10

PALPABLE

_____

_____

_____

_____

_____

_____

_____

_____

_____

Answers

Anagram Puzzle #1

aga	gnar	ora	porn
agar	goa	organ	prang
ago	gor	pagan	prao
agon	gorp	pan	pro
agora	gran	pang	proa
ana	grana	ang	prog
anoa	groan	panga	prong
apron	nag	par	rag
argon	nap	para	raga
gan	nog	parang	ran
gap	nor	pargo	rang
gar	oar	pong	rap
			roan

Anagram Puzzle #2

ado	duro	rads	sord
ados	duros	ras	sou
ads	oar	road	sour
aurous	oars	roads	sura
dor	ods	rod	surd
dors	ora	rods	udo
dorsa	orad	sad	udos
dos	ors	sard	urd
dour	oud	sarod	urds
doura	ouds	soar	ursa
duo	our	sod	urus
duos	ours	soda	
dura	rad	sora	

Anagram Puzzle #3

adds	dins	ads	did
aids	nidi	aid	din
ains	nisi	ain	dis
ands	said	ais	ids
anis	sain	and	ins
dads	sand	ani	sad
dais	add	dad	sin

Anagram Puzzle #4

fil	ifs	silt	tuis
fils	its	sit	uts
fist	lift	slit	wilt
fit	lifts	slut	wilts
fits	lis	suit	wis
flit	list	swift	wist
flits	lit	til	wit
flu	litu	tils	wits
flus	lust	tis	
fusil	sift	tui	

Anagram Puzzle #5

aid	dev	ire	ride
aide	deva	ired	rive
aider	die	rad	rived
air	dire	raid	vair
aired	diva	rave	var
aiver	dive	raved	via
are	diver	read	vide
arid	drive	red	vie
aver	ear	redia	vied
avid	era	rei	vier
dare	idea	rev	
dear	irade	rid	

Anagram Puzzle #6

adit	derat	ired	tare
aid	die	rad	tared
aide	diet	raid	tea
aider	dire	rat	tear
air	dirt	rate	ted
aired	dit	rated	terai
airt	dita	read	tide
airted	dite	red	tie
ait	drat	redia	tied
are	ear	rei	tier
arid	eat	ret	tire
art	edit	retia	tired
ate	era	rid	trad
dare	eta	ride	trade
dart	idea	rite	tread
date	irade	tad	triad
dater	irate	tae	tried
dear	ire	tar	

Anagram Puzzle #7

abed	beam	dame	lead
able	bed	deal	led
alb	bel	deb	mabe
ale	beldam	del	mad
amble	bema	eld	made
ambled	blade	elm	male
bad	blae	lab	mead
bade	blam	lad	meal
bal	blame	lade	med
bald	blamed	lam	medal
bale	bled	lamb	mel
baled	dab	lambed	meld
balm	dal	lame	
bam	dale	lamed	
bead	dam	lea	

Anagram Puzzle #8

all	coals	loca	sall
alls	col	local	salol
als	cola	locals	sau
also	colas	locus	scull
call	cols	oca	sol
calls	cos	ocas	sola
callus	cull	olla	sou
caul	culls	ollas	soul
cauls	lac	sac	sulcal
coal	lacs	sal	

Anagram Puzzle #9

abri	bard	dib	lib
aid	bid	dirl	libra
ail	bird	drab	lid
air	birl	drail	lidar
alb	bra	drib	lira
arb	brad	lab	rabid
arid	braid	lad	rad
aril	brail	laid	raid
bad	bridal	lair	rail
bail	dab	laird	rial
bal	dal	lard	rib
bald	darb	lari	rid
bar	dial	liar	

Anagram Puzzle #10

aba	apple	lab	pall
able	baa	label	palp
ala	baal	lap	palpal
alb	bal	lapel	pap
alba	bale	lea	papa
ale	ball	leal	papal
all	bap	leap	pea
alp	bel	paella	peal
ape	bell	pal	pep
appall	blae	pale	plea
appeal	ell	palea	pleb

6▶ Acrostics

In this chapter, you will use your knowledge of a PSAT/SAT vocabulary word's meaning to create a fun acrostic poem. This activity will also help you remember the spelling of each vocabulary word by breaking it down to create a poem.

Instructions

An acrostic poem begins with a word as its subject. The word is written vertically, from top to bottom, and each line of the poem begins with a different letter from the subject word. You can make this poem rhyme if you like, but rhyming is not necessary. In fact, lines could be made up of just one word, if you like.

Here is an example of an acrostic using the word **school**:

S tudying hard in each of our subjects
C lasses can be easy or hard, fun or tedious
H ow will we get all this homework done?
O ur teachers guide us through lectures and assignments
O ften we wait until the last minute to cram
L earning what we need to know for the future

Notice how each line in the acrostic has something to do with the subject word—**school**. When completing the following acrostics, make sure that each line refers back to the subject word. This will help you to remember its meaning when you're taking the PSAT or SAT exam.

Remember, there are no right or wrong answers for this game, so be as clever and creative as you like. Write whatever helps you remember each definition—and have fun!

Acrostic #1: RESPITE

Definition: a rest or break.
(Example: I deserve a *respite* after all this studying.)

R _____
E _____
S _____
P _____
I _____
T _____
E _____

Acrostic #2: SPARSE

Definition: thin, or few and scattered.
(Example: My math teacher is almost completely bald, except for a few *sparse* hairs combed across the top of his head.)

S _____
P _____
A _____
R _____
S _____
E _____

Acrostic #3: PLACID

Definition: serene or undisturbed.
(Example: In early spring, the lake water is so *placid* I can see my reflection.)

P _____
L _____
A _____
C _____
I _____
D _____

Acrostic #4: NOXIOUS

Definition: harmful or destructive.
(Example: I think it's time to clean my room—my closet is starting to give off a *noxious* odor again.)

N _____
O _____
X _____
I _____
O _____
U _____
S _____

Acrostic #5: BAUBLE

Definition: a trinket or other cheap ornament.
(Example: People like to collect beads, plastic rings, and other **baubles** at the Mardi Gras parade.)

B _____
A _____
U _____
B _____
L _____
E _____

Acrostic #6: COMELY

Definition: pleasing or attractive.
(Example: My little sister is so **comely** and charming, it's hard for my grandparents to refuse her requests.)

C _____
O _____
M _____
E _____
L _____
Y _____

Acrostic #7: TRITE

Definition: unoriginal or boring because of overuse.
(Example: I thought he was a clever speaker, but my teacher thought his arguments were *trite* and commonplace.)

T _____
R _____
I _____
T _____
E _____

Acrostic #8: SUPPRESS

Definition: to keep down or make it a secret.
(Example: She's such a natural gossip that it's hard for her to *suppress* any juicy news she hears.)

S _____
U _____
P _____
P _____
R _____
E _____
S _____
S _____

Acrostic #9: LEVITY

Definition: humor or frivolity.
(Example: The movie is over three hours long, and there's hardly any *levity* to lighten the viewing experience.)

L _____
E _____
V _____
I _____
T _____
Y _____

Acrostic #10: FILIAL

Definition: referring to the child-parent relationship.
(Example: I did my chores this week out of a *filial* obligation, rather than any real desire to make sure the dishes were washed and the carpets were clean.)

F _____
I _____
L _____
I _____
A _____
L _____

Answers

Answers will vary; a sample answer is below.

Acrostic #1: RESPITE

R elaxing after all this hard work
E njoying a break
S uspension of studying for a little while
P ostponement of practicing for the SAT
I ntermission from the grind
T aking time off
E nding the SAT study for a little while

7 ▶ Jumbles

In this chapter, you will learn to spell PSAT/ SAT words by rearranging the letters to discover vocabulary words. This will also help you to remember the definitions of these words, because they are linked by common subjects.

Instructions

Unscramble the words in each jumble by placing one letter in each box to spell PSAT/SAT vocabulary words.

If you need help, a list containing all the words used in this chapter can be found on page 71. Scan the list to see if you can identify the word(s) you're looking for. If you're completely stumped, give yourself a break by turning to another game or doing something else for a while. You can always come back and finish another time.

Answers to all the puzzles can be found at the end of the chapter— but don't peek until you've given each game your very best shot!

Jumble #1: Know-It-All

Hint: This jumble is made up of words that can be used to describe someone who is exceptionally wise or important.

AOGCUSSAI ☐☐☐☐☐☐☐☐☐

MNENTEI ☐☐☐☐☐☐☐

AYRMINUL ☐☐☐☐☐☐☐☐

ASENTPI ☐☐☐☐☐☐☐

PPSRIOSCUCIAE ☐☐☐☐☐☐☐☐☐☐☐☐☐

BERELAVNE ☐☐☐☐☐☐☐☐☐

Jumble #2: Nighty-Night

Hint: The words in this game are ones that you'd hear in the evening or nighttime hours.

ARCTLEGIH ☐☐☐☐☐☐☐☐☐

ULAOCTNNR ☐☐☐☐☐☐☐☐☐

ACOLHYN ☐☐☐☐☐☐☐

EOSPER ☐☐☐☐☐☐

ALQRIUTN ☐☐☐☐☐☐☐☐

ENWA ☐☐☐☐

Jumble #3: Past Tense

Hint: These words describe things that are going…going…gone.

CACHIRA ☐☐☐☐☐☐☐

OETSOELB ☐☐☐☐☐☐☐☐

ONSCMNARHAI ☐☐☐☐☐☐☐☐☐☐☐

EIVRMALP ☐☐☐☐☐☐☐☐

IGSEETV ☐☐☐☐☐☐☐

TRAFICTA ☐☐☐☐☐☐☐☐

Jumble #4: Our Daily Bread

Hint: This game comprises words that you might use when talking about eating and drinking.

MIEIBB ☐☐☐☐☐☐

SLUTOGUONT ☐☐☐☐☐☐☐☐☐☐

IULOBUBS ☐☐☐☐☐☐☐☐

AMFISH ☐☐☐☐☐☐

AGONFRIG ☐☐☐☐☐☐☐☐

ANMODGUR ☐☐☐☐☐☐☐☐

Jumble #5: Too Cool for School

Hint: The answers below are words you might hear while you're in the classroom.

DICTIACD ☐☐☐☐☐☐☐☐

DIEMRELA ☐☐☐☐☐☐☐☐

RUDEITE ☐☐☐☐☐☐☐

METO ☐☐☐☐

BIRDAGE ☐☐☐☐☐☐☐

REELCARB ☐☐☐☐☐☐☐☐

Jumble #6: Not My Favorite Guy

Hint: You might use the words below when talking about someone with whom you just don't get along.

BGTRAGAR ☐☐☐☐☐☐☐☐

ROBO ☐☐☐☐

RUSHLICH ☐☐☐☐☐☐☐☐

VANKE ☐☐☐☐☐

RUNCUTLET ☐☐☐☐☐☐☐☐☐

GAOICUSNUP ☐☐☐☐☐☐☐☐☐☐

Jumble #7: If You're Happy and You Know It

Hint: These are words you might use to describe your mood when you're really happy.

ADTEEL   ☐☐☐☐☐☐

OVALJI   ☐☐☐☐☐☐

BUNTJAIL   ☐☐☐☐☐☐☐☐

TLBHEI   ☐☐☐☐☐☐

FTCFRVEEEENS   ☐☐☐☐☐☐☐☐☐☐☐☐

TACCSEIT   ☐☐☐☐☐☐☐☐

Jumble #8: Enough Already!

Hint: You might use these words to describe something that's over the top.

SOBABITCM   ☐☐☐☐☐☐☐☐☐

IEFFVUES   ☐☐☐☐☐☐☐☐

NOEASIDRG   ☐☐☐☐☐☐☐☐☐

NOTUTTIESASO   ☐☐☐☐☐☐☐☐☐☐☐☐

LIDROF   ☐☐☐☐☐☐

SESRULUOFPU   ☐☐☐☐☐☐☐☐☐☐☐

Jumble #9: Puttin' on the Ritz

Hint: When you're showing how sophisticated you are, you might use these words.

OLOOTMAPNICS ⬜⬜⬜⬜⬜⬜⬜⬜⬜⬜⬜

EELIT ⬜⬜⬜⬜⬜

ETELNEG ⬜⬜⬜⬜⬜⬜⬜

SLABE ⬜⬜⬜⬜⬜

ROCSOEDU ⬜⬜⬜⬜⬜⬜⬜⬜

SPURETENTIO ⬜⬜⬜⬜⬜⬜⬜⬜⬜⬜

Jumble #10: Color My World

Hint: You might use the words in this game when decorating or talking about interior design.

HARSING ⬜⬜⬜⬜⬜⬜⬜

EPLUNTO ⬜⬜⬜⬜⬜⬜⬜

LIBHESLEM ⬜⬜⬜⬜⬜⬜⬜⬜⬜

DUDRAETSNET ⬜⬜⬜⬜⬜⬜⬜⬜⬜⬜

CELBECMAIP ⬜⬜⬜⬜⬜⬜⬜⬜⬜

OUPJESTAX ⬜⬜⬜⬜⬜⬜⬜⬜⬜

Word List for Chapter 7

abridge	ecstatic	grandiose	pretentious
anachronism	effervescent	halcyon	primeval
archaic	effusive	imbibe	pugnacious
artifact	elated	impeccable	remedial
bibulous	elite	jovial	repose
blasé	embellish	jubilant	sagacious
blithe	eminent	juxtapose	sapient
bombastic	erudite	knave	superfluous
boor	famish	lethargic	tome
braggart	florid	luminary	tranquil
cerebral	foraging	nocturnal	truculent
churlish	garnish	obsolete	understated
cosmopolitan	genteel	opulent	venerable
decorous	gluttonous	ostentatious	vestige
didactic	gourmand	perspicacious	wane

Answers

Jumble #1: Know-It-All

A O G C U S S A I	**SAGACIOUS**
M N E N T E I	**EMINENT**
A Y R M I N U L	**LUMINARY**
A S E N T P I	**SAPIENT**
P P S R I O S C U C I A E	**PERSPICACIOUS**
B E R E L A V N E	**VENERABLE**

Jumble #2: Nighty-Night

A R C T L E G I H	**LETHARGIC**
U L A O C T N N R	**NOCTURNAL**
A C O L H Y N	**HALCYON**
E O S P E R	**REPOSE**
A L Q R I U T N	**TRANQUIL**
E N W A	**WANE**

Jumble #3: Past Tense

C A C H I R A	**ARCHAIC**
O E T S O E L B	**OBSOLETE**
O N S C M N A R H A I	**ANACHRONISM**
E I V R M A L P	**PRIMEVAL**
I G S E E T V	**VESTIGE**
T R A F I C T A	**ARTIFACT**

Jumble #4: Our Daily Bread

M I E I B B	**IMBIBE**
S L U T O G U O N T	**GLUTTONOUS**
I U L O B U B S	**BIBULOUS**
A M F I S H	**FAMISH**
A G O N F R I G	**FORAGING**
A N M O D G U R	**GOURMAND**

Jumble #5: Too Cool for School

D I C T I A C D	**DIDACTIC**
D I E M R E L A	**REMEDIAL**
R U D E I T E	**ERUDITE**
M E T O	**TOME**
B I R D A G E	**ABRIDGE**
R E E L C A R B	**CEREBRAL**

Jumble #6: Not My Favorite Guy

B G T R A G A R	**BRAGGART**
R O B O	**BOOR**
R U S H L I C H	**CHURLISH**
V A N K E	**KNAVE**
R U N C U T L E T	**TRUCULENT**
G A O I C U S N U P	**PUGNACIOUS**

Jumble #7: If You're Happy and You Know It

A D T E E L	**ELATED**
O V A L J I	**JOVIAL**
B U N T J A I L	**JUBILANT**
T L B H E I	**BLITHE**
F T C F R V E E E E N S	**EFFERVESCENT**
T A C C S E I T	**ECSTATIC**

Jumble #8: Enough Already!

S O B A B I T C M	**BOMBASTIC**
I E F F V U E S	**EFFUSIVE**
N O E A S I D R G	**GRANDIOSE**
N O T U T T I E S A S O	**OSTENTATIOUS**
L I D R O F	**FLORID**
S E S R U L U O F P U	**SUPERFLUOUS**

Jumble #9: Puttin' on the Ritz

OLOOTMAPNICS	**COSMOPOLITAN**
EELIT	**ELITE**
ETELNEG	**GENTEEL**
SLABE	**BLASE**
ROCSOEDU	**DECOROUS**
SPURETENTIO	**PRETENTIOUS**

Jumble #10: Color My World

HARSING	**GARNISH**
EPLUNTO	**OPULENT**
LIBHESLEM	**EMBELLISH**
DUDRAETSNET	**UNDERSTATED**
CELBECMAIP	**IMPECCABLE**
OUPJESTAX	**JUXTAPOSE**

8 ▶ Word Searches

In this chapter, you will reinforce your ability to recognize PSAT/SAT vocabulary words by finding them in the following word search puzzles.

Instructions

Each word on the right side of the puzzle is hidden somewhere within the letters on the left side. Words will be found exactly as they are spelled, but may be written left to right, right to left, up and down, or diagonally.

Answers are found at the end of the chapter. Be sure to look up any unfamiliar words in the glossary at the back of the book; it's not enough to know how the words are spelled—you will also need to know their meanings when you take the PSAT or SAT exam!

Word Search Game #1

```
C K J N J L Q B Y Y C S N P U
O B S U O I G E R G E S R O P
M G S J A Y O R S U Y O E E O
W U T O P I A Q A G X L M Q V
O G B F R S I Z D I B D Y O X
O T Y G F D C B M A G O V R G
I G D W S C F I T Y E S J U T
O I L T N U T C N E M O F G C
U C K C O Y A V S T Q A G L E
S L X F Y R T A D Y I R M Z D
W A M R T Q L W M K O L F B F
X N M P V I E L B A E L L A M
L Y F D E E Z I A T D K J A B
K T I N E T A N I M U R H X E
H F T A I G N O M I N I O U S
```

SALIENT
PROXIMITY
ODIOUS
IGNOMINIOUS
EGREGIOUS
TRACTABLE
MALLEABLE
SCINTILLA
UTOPIA
RUMINATE

Word Search Game #2

```
S M N S U K P E T D H A K F Y
B W D S L H A Z N Y X J W L Y
N Z N Y B S R I E S C K F X B
N U C C I U A T I Y E Q Y H F
J V H G E O D A S C L Y O Q O
O D A X L M O K N N B V T F E
C Y L I B I X O A X B E B T S
U R A X A N U Q R B I S D A O
L A N X T A T T T X U Q C T A
A T T U U N L T B J Q Q K C Q
R U F I F G Q L U E O U T L P
P L R H E A Q E I O N A A Y D
Q A Z D R M O S G V E I Z L E
S S F X R I S V Q Z O M G U M
B W R Q I C R N W J C M M N X
```

SALUTARY
JOCULAR
PARADOX
IRREFUTABLE
NONCHALANT
QUALM
MAGNANIMOUS
TRANSIENT
QUIBBLE
BENIGN

Word Search Game #3

```
G K R G T M P O P E M H J M K
L R F T F D E T R I T U S I K
X N E I B I J L V I X X S O W
O N E L Y X I I N G O N M W J
O G O O V R D E F A U I T S Q
I X H T P W Z N D D E E E F F
S Y R X N H L A D X T K D V O
V V E Y L A Y X P T A O A P B
R I E T T V W T O P L Y L W J
S K O S Y B Z R E D L I O I U
A P X E O M N D L P I Z C L O
S M G V I Z A Q Y Q C T E Y E
B G V A H T Z M B J S Z A Z O
F Y S R T W H W V X O A S W Q
M X I T Y Z E A L O T P R W U
```

TRAVESTY

ACCOLADE

ZENITH

NEOPHYTE

ZEALOT

WILY

YOKE

OSCILLATE

WANTON

DETRITUS

Word Search Game #4

```
R M F T Y O I V Y Z P I O R V
D I Y X H K M B M H Y I Q B M
Z L X T I T P O G K W Q V Z B
F I J U D F E A P A T O I T I
Z E V I S U R T B O G V J V I
D U C N K R V F S G A M B O L
T T P C O P I S L K Y V F U K
X D X T U L O N L H Z F I E T
C Q E C A C U M E N C G I G X
J G K Q S H S U P F E G V D X
M O Q O T W V Q K U M S U Q Y
Y F E F C O N D U C I V E M E
H B L B L A S R E V I N U Y T
D Y J H Z K T N E G N I R T S
S B T I L T J U H Z N X J D Q
```

IMPERVIOUS

UNIVERSAL

STRINGENT

GAMBOL

OBTRUSIVE

IOTA

GARROTE

ACUMEN

CONDUCIVE

MILIEU

Word Search Game #5

```
I N A W B J Q R X D H B X F N
T J X F F O A W V W D K E C T
Y G N M R K T U B B Y W X J T
Z X C I E D E P M I X R A T W
T R L Q S R P V J A X L J R U
Y R A D N A U Q P I E E G M Y
X Y S R U N N E I C H L T E D
M O C P G O J G E C E B P U C
M O H T A F P J E D Z I L L M
C Z M U T C I D R R I L K U G
R L I Q C U K V P J M L Y C P
T A A N O S T A L G I A F M G
D T Q K Y N R Z Y K Q F N F W
K U P R U D E N C E N N P E R
Q A Q T T N A E R C S I M E X
```

MISCREANT
WARY
PRUDENCE
QUANDARY
NOSTALGIA
FATHOM
GERMANE
DICTUM
FALLIBLE
IMPEDE

Word Search Game #6

```
M I J A L Q W G B B L G H B Q
X D M F T F J T X R O I O D Y
R M E M O S N I W A F L X U H
Q A Q L V O Y Z L B N F F T S
E B D B O P R U S U O O C D X
E A R E G Y R E N A C I H C J
R S A L T W K U F A D C U X F
X H S I Q A J I B E M L B D I
P E D E Y T C Z B M C M D S T
G D D Z A E V O Q K U J U H G
Q G B K Q O V I V U Q C Y Z X
V Y H I E Q W R Q I E U C U O
L R Q A N I Q Y U D U U K U D
J F T S H I P R M P M Q E X S
V L L O U M E H N Z K S E A E
```

ABASHED
USURP
WINSOME
CHICANERY
SUCCUMB
BELIE
EDICT
QUEUE
PURVEY
EQUIVOCATE

Word Search Game #7

```
K  S  V  O  I  L  G  O  R  B  M  I  Q  C  H
S  C  O  N  V  I  V  I  A  L  U  L  F  E  A
T  J  W  R  Q  S  L  Y  B  Z  F  P  V  N  A
B  H  Q  Q  L  F  L  J  N  M  S  A  Z  E  O
F  M  H  B  E  G  G  U  R  H  S  P  D  E  W
D  A  E  R  K  O  P  V  H  I  B  T  J  L  E
W  L  U  C  U  J  A  V  V  A  U  Q  D  Y  L
V  D  S  L  N  C  P  E  L  M  J  L  Y  H  S
Y  E  H  B  L  E  V  I  A  T  H  A  N  D  R
P  B  T  O  C  I  D  G  N  N  Q  N  I  A  E
L  R  I  J  C  J  I  E  H  R  M  Z  T  B  N
R  G  D  Z  E  A  B  S  R  I  X  D  X  O  I
T  R  A  N  S  C  E  N  D  C  P  I  D  R  G
S  E  L  F  N  C  T  I  C  A  T  Y  T  O  M
I  D  E  A  D  A  I  Q  H  H  E  Z  I  G  A
```

ENIGMA
IMBROGLIO
TACIT
CREDENCE
BEDLAM
EVASIVE
CONVIVIAL
GAMUT
LEVIATHAN
TRANSCEND

Word Search Game #8

```
S  P  M  A  D  L  A  B  I  R  U  W  H  M  N
R  L  Q  A  E  N  L  U  I  U  S  L  D  C  P
B  H  W  B  S  T  A  T  R  J  U  B  D  M  G
D  B  P  M  D  T  A  R  K  J  O  V  B  Z  J
O  U  Z  N  W  L  O  N  A  R  L  E  H  E  O
D  H  C  D  T  K  F  L  A  U  U  Z  I  M  T
O  A  H  E  A  P  J  R  F  M  M  Y  I  O  I
H  B  I  O  Q  T  Y  R  R  P  E  P  D  S  I
T  F  D  Z  F  P  K  E  E  Z  R  H  K  I  Y
B  X  E  D  U  T  I  P  R  U  T  D  R  O  W
U  M  W  M  G  S  G  G  J  S  M  D  E  N  I
N  K  D  I  L  A  N  A  B  L  K  G  K  G  T
E  U  Q  I  L  B  O  S  Z  I  Q  Q  S  X  S
R  V  L  B  S  U  O  T  I  U  Q  I  B  U  E
M  Z  E  O  V  Z  V  E  J  B  L  N  O  A  M
```

TREMULOUS
RIBALD
CHIDE
UBIQUITOUS
FLOTSAM
TURPITUDE
OBLIQUE
BANAL
NOISOME
EMANATE

Word Search Game #9

```
L P Z W F J M H W T U W B F W
F H G G H N K X I V T E Y S F
V B J P S S E R G S N A R T Q
D L A N G U I D E W E G H A R
K I R X O J X E J T L E I D Z
E J Q I Y A B T S Y O S R X E
E V X B J M S A A T V T S K I
F H W P B W L I L I E I U G S
K B T R D C V T J C N C T T G
O I Z H O D B A D A E U E A V
Z L L N T A T S O N B L N K K
E F O Y U A S W X E G A U V C
O C Q G B V R P P T X T J E M
I I N M V Y P W M D U E B E A
P A J Q R Q F Z Y G O L A N A
```

TRANSGRESS
WRATH
SATIATE
HIRSUTE
BENEVOLENT
ANALOGY
GESTICULATE
LANGUID
TENACITY
ICONOCLAST

Word Search Game #10

```
C G G Q W R K U S S E R G E H
V S U O I N E G N I Q R T N C
N K Z E I T G E I S T N F B Z
U G N L T D K K M S U C H E K
I G A I N J V A A O U C B Q Y
I V W C E M V R M J R J A C Q
B D H O M I F A O K R V Y T N
Q X J D A Y T M E D I O C R E
X O W Q L N U D J E Q A E S L
E V I T A R C U L M V X I T S
F Y P T E I R E T O S E X N D
O C Z D R T P Y K A R T R N K
C X A G O T F P U G S D B O L
N B T C B X U G A K O T S N U
B C B Q C H A U N E G A M O H
```

MEDIOCRE
ZEITGEIST
EGRESS
TANTAMOUNT
LUCRATIVE
HOMAGE
ESOTERIC
INGENIOUS
DOCILE
LAMENT

Answers

Word Search Game #1

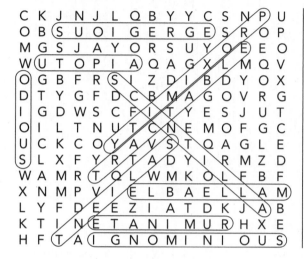

SALIENT

PROXIMITY

ODIOUS

IGNOMINIOUS

EGREGIOUS

TRACTABLE

MALLEABLE

SCINTILLA

UTOPIA

RUMINATE

Word Search Game #2

SALUTARY

JOCULAR

PARADOX

IRREFUTABLE

NONCHALANT

QUALM

MAGNANIMOUS

TRANSIENT

QUIBBLE

BENIGN

Word Search Game #3

```
G K R G T M P O P E M H J M K
L R F T F D E T R I T U S I K
X N E I B I J L V I X X S O W
O N E L Y X I I N G O N M W J
O G O O V R D E F A U I T S Q
I X H T P W Z N D D E E E F F
S Y R X N H L A D X T K D V O
V V E Y L A Y X P T A O A P B
R I E T T V W T O P L Y L J J
S K O S Y B Z R E D L I O C U
A P X E O M N D L P I Z C C O
S M G V I Z A Q Y Q C T C A E
B G V A H T Z M B J S Z A Z O
F Y S R T W H W V X O A S W Q
M X I T Y Z E A L O T P R W U
```

TRAVESTY
ACCOLADE
ZENITH
NEOPHYTE
ZEALOT
WILY
YOKE
OSCILLATE
WANTON
DETRITUS

Word Search Game #4

```
R M F T Y O I V Y Z P I O R V
D I Y X H K M B M H Y I Q B M
Z L X T I T P O G K W Q V Z B
F I J U D F E A P A T O I T I
Z E V I S U R T B O G V J V I
D U C N K R V F S G A M B O L
T T P C O P I S L K Y V F U K
X D X T U L O N L H Z F I E T
C Q E C A C U M E N C G I G X
J G K Q S H S U P F E G V D X
M O Q O T W V Q K U M S U Q Y
Y F E F C O N D U C I V E M E
H B L B L A S R E V I N U Y T
D Y J H Z K T N E G N I R T S
S B T I L T J U H Z N X J D Q
```

IMPERVIOUS
UNIVERSAL
STRINGENT
GAMBOL
OBTRUSIVE
IOTA
GARROTE
ACUMEN
CONDUCIVE
MILIEU

Word Search Game #5

```
I   N   A   W   B   J   Q   R   X   D   H   B   X   F   N
T   J   X   F   F   O   A   W   V   W   D   K   E   C   T
Y   G   N   M   R   K   T   U   B   B   Y   W   X   J   T
Z   X   C   I   E   D   E   P   M   I   X   R   A   T   W
T   R   L   Q   S   R   P   V   J   A   X   L   J   R   U
Y   R   A   D   N   A   U   Q   P   I   E   E   G   M   Y
X   Y   S   R   U   N   N   E   I   C   H   L   T   E   D
M   O   C   P   G   O   J   G   E   C   E   B   P   U   C
M   O   H   T   A   F   P   J   E   D   Z   I   L   L   M
C   Z   M   U   T   C   I   D   R   R   I   L   K   U   G
R   L   I   Q   C   U   K   V   P   J   M   L   Y   C   P
T   A   A   N   O   S   T   A   L   G   I   A   F   M   G
D   T   Q   K   Y   N   R   Z   Y   K   Q   F   N   F   W
K   U   P   R   U   D   E   N   C   E   N   N   P   E   R
Q   A   Q   T   T   N   A   E   R   C   S   I   M   E   X
```

MISCREANT
WARY
PRUDENCE
QUANDARY
NOSTALGIA
FATHOM
GERMANE
DICTUM
FALLIBLE
IMPEDE

Word Search Game #6

```
M   I   J   A   L   Q   W   G   B   B   L   G   H   B   Q
X   D   M   F   T   F   J   T   X   R   O   I   O   D   Y
R   M   E   M   O   S   N   I   W   A   F   L   X   U   H
Q   A   Q   L   V   O   Y   Z   L   B   N   F   F   T   S
E   B   D   B   O   P   R   U   S   U   O   O   C   D   X
E   A   R   E   G   Y   R   E   N   A   C   I   H   C   J
R   S   A   L   T   W   K   U   F   A   D   C   U   X   F
X   H   S   I   Q   A   J   I   B   E   M   L   B   D   I
P   E   D   E   Y   T   C   Z   B   M   C   M   D   S   T
G   D   D   Z   A   E   V   O   Q   K   U   J   U   H   G
Q   G   B   K   Q   O   V   I   V   U   Q   C   Y   Z   X
V   Y   H   I   E   Q   W   R   Q   I   E   U   C   U   O
L   R   Q   A   N   I   Q   Y   U   D   U   U   K   U   D
J   F   T   S   H   I   P   R   M   P   M   Q   E   X   S
V   L   L   O   U   M   E   H   N   Z   K   S   E   A   E
```

ABASHED
USURP
WINSOME
CHICANERY
SUCCUMB
BELIE
EDICT
QUEUE
PURVEY
EQUIVOCATE

Word Search Game #7

K S V O I L G O R B M I Q C H
S C O N V I V I A L U L F E A
T J W R Q S L Y B Z F P V N A
B H Q Q L F L J N M S A Z E O
F M H B E G G U R H S P D E W
D A E R K O P V H I B T J L E
W L U C U J A V V A U Q D Y L
V D S L N C P E L M J L Y H S
Y E H B L E V I A T H A N D R
P B T O C I D G N N Q N I A E
L R I J C J I E H R M Z T B N
R G D Z E A B S R I X D X O I
T R A N S C E N D C P I D R G
S E L F N C T I C A T Y T O M
I D E A D A I Q H H E Z I G A

ENIGMA
IMBROGLIO
TACIT
CREDENCE
BEDLAM
EVASIVE
CONVIVIAL
GAMUT
LEVIATHAN
TRANSCEND

Word Search Game #8

S P M A D L A B I R U W H M N
R L Q A E N L U I U S L D C P
B H W B S T A T R J U B D M G
D B P M D T A R K J O V B Z J
O U Z N W L O N A R L E H E O
D H C D T K F L A U U Z I M T
O A H E A P J R F M M Y I O I
H B I O Q T Y R R P E P D S I
T F D Z F P K E E Z R H K I Y
B X E D U T I P R U T D R O W
U M W M G S G G J S M D E N I
N K D I L A N A B L K G K G T
E U Q I L B O S Z I Q Q S X S
R V L B S U O T I U Q I B U E
M Z E O V Z V E J B L N O A M

TREMULOUS
RIBALD
CHIDE
UBIQUITOUS
FLOTSAM
TURPITUDE
OBLIQUE
BANAL
NOISOME
EMANATE

Word Search Game #9

```
L P Z W F J M H W T U W B F W
F H G G H N K X I V T E Y S F
V B J P S S E R G S N A R T Q
D L A N G U I D E W E G H A R
K I R X O J X E J T L E I D Z
E J Q I Y A B T S Y O S R X E
E V X B J M S A A T V T S K I
F H W P B W L I L I E I U G S
K B T R D C V T J C N C T T G
O I Z H O D B A D A E U E A V
Z L L N T A T S O N B L N K K
E F O Y U A S W X E G A U V C
O C Q G B V R P P X A T J E M
I I N M V Y P W M D U E B E A
P A J Q R Q F Z Y G O L A N A
```

TRANSGRESS
WRATH
SATIATE
HIRSUTE
BENEVOLENT
ANALOGY
GESTICULATE
LANGUID
TENACITY
ICONOCLAST

Word Search Game #10

```
C G G Q W R K U S S E R G E H
V S U O I N E G N I Q R T N C
N K Z E I T G E I S T N F B Z
U G N L T D K K M S U C H E K
I G A I N J V A A O U C B Q Y
I V W C E M V R M J R J A C Q
B D H O M I F A O K R V Y T N
Q X J D A Y T M E D I O C R E
X O W Q L N U D J E Q A E S L
E V I T A R C U L M V X I T S
F Y P T C I R E T O S E X N D
O C Z D R T P Y K A R T R N K
C X A G O T F P U G S D B O L
N B T C B X U G A K O T S N U
B C B Q C H A U N E G A M O H
```

MEDIOCRE
ZEITGEIST
EGRESS
TANTAMOUNT
LUCRATIVE
HOMAGE
ESOTERIC
INGENIOUS
DOCILE
LAMENT

9 ▶ Matching Column Games

In this chapter, you'll learn to look carefully at similar sounding (or similarly spelled) pairs of words to find the correct meaning for each.

Instructions

Draw a line to match each word in Column A with its definition in Column B. Be careful—these lists are made up of pairs of commonly confused words, and the games can be a little challenging.

Answers can be found at the end of the chapter.

Matching Column Game #1

Column A	Column B
allusion	practicing extreme self-denial
illusion	location, scene, or point of occurrence
aesthetic	expression of respect or affection; good wishes
ascetic	something that is misleading or deceptive
cite	occurring at the same time; running parallel
site	appreciation of beauty or art
compliment	indirect reference
complement	refer to or quote authoritatively; call upon officially
concurrent	following one after the other in order
consecutive	make something complete

Matching Column Game #2

Column A	Column B
connote	modest; having good moral judgment
denote	indifferent; not interested
discrete	someone who settles in a new country
discreet	associate; express indirectly or imply
disinterested	glue-like; gummy
uninterested	indicate; make known
emigrant	having an enormous appetite
immigrant	separate; individually distinct
glutinous	one who departs a country to settle elsewhere
gluttonous	impartial; unbiased

Matching Column Game #3

Column A	Column B
figuratively	symbolically; metaphorically
literally	toward the front; send on or pass along
foreword	writing materials; notepaper
forward	form; produce; create
stationary	unlawful
stationery	actually; word-for-word
comprise	to draw out (especially emotion or information)
compose	made up of; included within a particular scope
elicit	introductory note or preface
illicit	fixed; unmoving

Matching Column Game #4

Column A	Column B
inflammable	capable of being bought; corrupt through bribery
nonflammable	one who founds or establishes; give way; sink
founder	next-to-last
flounder	most remote; last; best or most extreme
penultimate	contrary or opposed; unfavorable
ultimate	having a feeling of intense dislike or repulsion
venial	unable to be set on fire
venal	minor; pardonable
adverse	able to be set on fire
averse	struggle or thrash about

Matching Column Game #5

Column A

empathy

sympathy

appraise

apprise

augur

auger

censure

censor

compare

contrast

Column B

give notice; tell

tool used for making holes or removing loose material

feeling of loyalty or support for another

one who supervises conduct or morals; to suppress

set a value or estimate the cost of something

official reprimand or condemnation

find similarities or resemblances

find a degree of difference

sharing another's emotions or feelings

a person who foretells events or sees the future

Matching Column Game #6

Column A

council

counsel

continuous

continual

decent

descent

defuse

diffuse

incidence

incidents

Column B

nonstop; continuing uninterrupted

an advisory or legislative body or group

recurring in rapid succession; occurring regularly

downward inclination; deriving from ancestors

advice, policy, or plan of action

make less harmful or tense

frequency of occurrence

happenings; events that lead to grave consequences

appropriate; free from immodesty or obscenity

not concentrated; spread out

Matching Column Game #7

Column A

insight

incite

ensure

insure

marital

martial

officious

official

perspicuous

perspicacious

Column B

provide or obtain insurance; take precaution

relating to an office or position

move to action; stir up

suited for war; related to military life

to make certain

transparent; clear and precise

of or relating to marriage

penetration; seeing the inner nature of something

kind; dutiful

acutely insightful and wise

Matching Column Game #8

Column A

proscribe

prescribe

precede

proceed

stature

statute

tortuous

torturous

vociferous

voracious

Column B

continue; follow a certain course

height; quality or status gained by development

recommend; specify with authority

twisting and turning; devious or indirect tactics

excessively greedy or eager; having a large appetite

unpleasant or painful

condemn or forbid as harmful

law or legislative act

be, go, or come ahead or in front of; surpass

blatant; conspicuous and offensive outcry

Matching Column Game #9

Column A	Column B
conscience	suggest; express or state indirectly
conscious	guess; deduce
eminent	awake; aware
imminent	able to be perceived or detected
imply	standing out or above in quality or position
infer	worthy of notice
notable	at hand; about to occur
noticeable	having no connection with an issue; unrelated
irreverent	moral sense of right and wrong
irrelevant	showing disrespect

Matching Column Game #10

Column A	Column B
convince	show off shamelessly
persuade	encourage; talk someone into something
flaunt	an educator in a position of high authority
flout	basic truth or belief; rule of personal conduct
principal	plead with; urge
principle	neither moral nor immoral
amoral	tease; taunt
immoral	to agree or be in accord
gibe	disregard; show scorn or contempt
jibe	unethical; morally objectionable

Answers

Matching Column Game #1

Column A

allusion
illusion
aesthetic

ascetic
cite

site
compliment
complement

concurrent
consecutive

Column B

practicing extreme self-denial
location, scene, or point of occurrence
expression of respect or affection; good
    wishes
something that is misleading or deceptive
occurring at the same time; running
    parallel
appreciation of beauty or art
indirect reference
refer to or quote authoritatively; call
    upon officially
following one after the other in order
make something complete

Matching Column Game #2

Column A

connote
denote
discrete
discreet
disinterested
uninterested
emigrant
immigrant
glutinous

gluttonous

Column B

modest; having good moral judgment
indifferent; not interested
someone who settles in a new country
associate; express indirectly or imply
glue-like; gummy
indicate; make known
having an enormous appetite
separate; individually distinct
one who departs a country to settle
    elsewhere
impartial; unbiased

Matching Column Game #3

Column A	Column B
figuratively	symbolically; metaphorically
literally	toward the front; send on or pass along
foreword	writing materials; notepaper
forward	form; produce; create
stationary	unlawful
stationery	actually; word-for-word
comprise	to draw out (especially emotion or information)
compose	made up of; included within a particular scope
elicit	introductory note or preface
illicit	fixed; unmoving

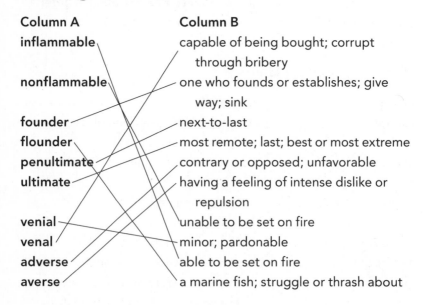

Matching Column Game #4

Column A	Column B
inflammable	capable of being bought; corrupt through bribery
nonflammable	one who founds or establishes; give way; sink
founder	next-to-last
flounder	most remote; last; best or most extreme
penultimate	contrary or opposed; unfavorable
ultimate	having a feeling of intense dislike or repulsion
venial	unable to be set on fire
venal	minor; pardonable
adverse	able to be set on fire
averse	a marine fish; struggle or thrash about

Matching Column Game #5

Column A
empathy
sympathy

appraise
apprise

augur

auger
censure
censor
compare
contrast

Column B
give notice; tell
tool used for making holes or removing loose material
feeling of loyalty or support for another
one who supervises conduct or morals; to suppress
set a value or estimate the cost of something
official reprimand or condemnation
find similarities or resemblances
find a degree of difference
sharing another's emotions or feelings
a person who foretells events or sees the future

Matching Column Game #6

Column A
council
counsel
continuous

continual

decent
descent
defuse
diffuse

incidence

incidents

Column B
nonstop; continuing uninterrupted
an advisory or legislative body or group
recurring in rapid succession; occurring regularly
downward inclination; deriving from ancestors
advice, policy, or plan of action
make less harmful or tense
frequency of occurrence
happenings; events that lead to grave consequences
appropriate; free from immodesty or obscenity
not concentrated; spread out

Matching Column Game #7

Column A	Column B
insight	provide or obtain insurance; take precaution
incite	relating to an office or position
ensure	move to action; stir up
insure	suited for war; related to military life
marital	to make certain
martial	transparent; clear and precise
officious	of or relating to marriage
official	penetration; seeing the inner nature of something
perspicuous	kind; dutiful
perspicacious	acutely insightful and wise

Matching Column Game #8

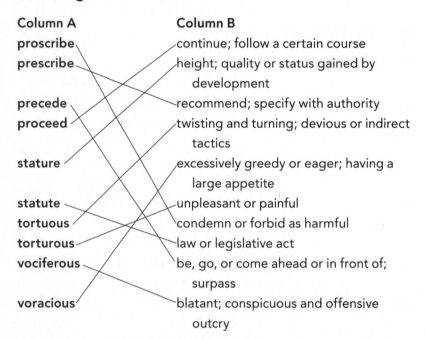

Column A	Column B
proscribe	continue; follow a certain course
prescribe	height; quality or status gained by development
precede	recommend; specify with authority
proceed	twisting and turning; devious or indirect tactics
stature	excessively greedy or eager; having a large appetite
statute	unpleasant or painful
tortuous	condemn or forbid as harmful
torturous	law or legislative act
vociferous	be, go, or come ahead or in front of; surpass
voracious	blatant; conspicuous and offensive outcry

Matching Column Game #9

Column A	Column B
conscience	suggest; express or state indirectly
conscious	guess; deduce
eminent	awake; aware
imminent	able to be perceived or detected
imply	standing out or above in quality or position
infer	worthy of notice
notable	at hand; about to occur
noticeable	having no connection with an issue; unrelated
irreverent	moral sense of right and wrong
irrelevant	showing disrespect

Matching Column Game #10

Column A	Column B
convince	show off shamelessly
persuade	encourage; talk someone into something
flaunt	an educator in a position of high authority
flout	basic truth or belief; rule of personal conduct
principal	plead with; urge
principle	neither moral nor immoral
amoral	tease; taunt
immoral	to agree or be in accord
gibe	disregard; show scorn or contempt
jibe	unethical; morally objectionable

10 ▶ Double-Word Puzzles

In this chapter, you will learn to remember definitions and spellings of PSAT/SAT words by identifying a word by its meaning, then spelling it out.

Instructions

Use the definitions provided to find each clue word. Write the word in the boxes next to each definition. Then unscramble the letters in the circled boxes within the clue words to discover the bonus vocabulary word.

If you get stuck, scan the word list on page 110 to see if you can figure out the word to match each definition. Be careful—some words in this chapter have similar definitions or spellings, and others have been used more than once.

Puzzle #1

1. noisy; unpleasant sounding (11 letters)

2. eliminate; obliterate (6 letters)

3. short-lived (9 letters)

4. impossible to understand (12 letters)

5. great anger; wrath (3 letters)

6. dreamy; without interest or enthusiasm (13 letters)

7. figurative; not literal (12 letters)

8. of or related to ships, navigation, or sailing (8 letters)

9. assuming too much (12 letters)

10. not strict; permissive (7 letters)

Bonus: fickle; changing on a whim

Puzzle #2

1. embankment or pier;
   (5 letters)

2. very expensive
   (11 letters)

3. most essential part
   (12 letters)

4. urge or force to action
   (5 letters)

5. something made up; lie;
   untruth (11 letters)

6. very clear and direct
   (8 letters)

7. dull; boring (7 letters)

8. abhorrence; dislike; disgust (6 letters)

9. wrong (9 letters)

10. thin; transparent
    (10 letters)

Bonus: lacking moral discipline
       or restraint; lewd

Puzzle #3

1. moral corruption
   (9 letters)

2. exact copy or reproduction (9 letters)

3. lie or relax in a warm
   environment; take
   pleasure or enjoyment
   (4 letters)

4. false; calculating
   (12 letters)

5. driven by lust (10 letters)

6. something that interferes
   with or delays action or
   progress (9 letters)

7. evil speech; curse
   (11 letters)

8. easily accomplished or
   attained (6 letters)

9. never giving up
   (11 letters)

10. refuse to accept
    (9 letters)

Bonus: undecided; unclear

Puzzle #4

1. summon or signal with an inviting wave or nod (6 letters)

2. echo (8 letters)

3. mild; moderate (9 letters)

4. impulsive (9 letters)

5. regard someone or something as perfect (8 letters)

6. something that interferes with or delays action or progress (9 letters)

7. adequate; sufficient (12 letters)

8. reserved; restrained; reluctant to talk or draw attention (8 letters)

9. shelf set above a fireplace (6 letters)

10. unselfish concern for others; self-sacrifice (8 letters)

Bonus: smug; self-satisfied

Puzzle #5

1. odd; not fitting a particular pattern (9 letters)

2. arrogant or haughty (12 letters)

3. trick (4 letters)

4. a typical example (7 letters)

5. event that occurs at a critical time (8 letters)

6. requiring much physical effort (9 letters)

7. praise, glorify, or honor (4 letters)

8. careful to consider all feelings and consequences; prudent (11 letters)

9. wrong (9 letters)

10. false; calculating (12 letters)

Bonus: doing only what is right or proper; having moral integrity

Puzzle #6

1. aggressively conceited and presumptuous (9 letters)

2. suspicious; fearful (12 letters)

3. unsophisticated; inexperienced (5 letters)

4. worship or adore unquestionably and to excess (7 letters)

5. being similar or comparable in nature (11 letters)

6. take the place of; serve as a substitute for (8 letters)

7. someone who travels from one region to another in search of work (7 letters)

8. quirk or unique trait (12 letters)

9. manner of walking or moving (4 letters)

10. obvious (7 letters)

Bonus: someone on foot, walking; unimaginative or boring

Puzzle #7

1. support (7 letters)

2. penetrate; understand; probe (6 letters)

3. wealthy elderly woman (7 letters)

4. clumsy or inexpert (5 letters)

5. based on guesswork; not proven (12 letters)

6. meant to be humorous or not taken seriously (9 letters)

7. weak; no longer strong or vital (6 letters)

8. aggression (12 letters)

9. without restraint (9 letters)

10. unwilling; reluctant (5 letters)

Bonus: odd mixture or combination

Puzzle #8

1. unjustified (11 letters)

2. shelf set above a fire-place (6 letters)

3. cause or bring into exis-tence (8 letters)

4. doubtful (7 letters)

5. loose robe (6 letters)

6. place where two or more things come together; being joined (8 letters)

7. penetration; seeing the inner nature of some-thing (7 letters)

8. driven by lust; lewd (10 letters)

9. using indecent or vul-gar language; obscene (10 letters)

10. moving or bending with ease (5 letters)

Bonus: speak out against someone or something

Puzzle #9

1. lacking in strength or firmness (3 letters)

2. take back (6 letters)

3. maze; complex system of paths or tunnels (9 letters)

4. deceptive; pretending to be good or virtuous (12 letters)

5. easily accomplished or attained (6 letters)

6. abundant (4 letters)

7. showing enthusiasm or exhilaration (9 letters)

8. to the side (7 letters)

9. result brought about by something else (6 letters)

10. compensation for a professional service (10 letters)

Bonus: to excite

Puzzle #10

1. cloak or cape as a symbol of authority (6 letters)

2. make a start; go on board (6 letters)

3. ill-tempered; cranky (12 letters)

4. favorable; fortunate (10 letters)

5. equal; believer in equality (11 letters)

6. sign; support (7 letters)

7. truthful or sincere; free from bias (6 letters)

8. showing esteem or respect (11 letters)

9. showing enthusiasm or exhilaration (9 letters)

10. lawful or valid (10 letters)

Bonus: revival

Word List for Chapter 10

altruism	effect	idiosyncrasy	mantel
ambivalent	effete	idolize	mantle
anomalous	egalitarian	impel	metaphorical
apprehensive	embark	impetuous	migrant
auspicious	endorse	imponderable	naive
bask	ephemeral	inept	nautical
beckon	epitome	insight	pedestrian
belligerence	erroneous	ire	presumptuous
blatant	exhilarate	junction	prohibitive
bolster	explicit	juncture	quintessence
bumptious	fabrication	kimono	repudiate
cacophonous	facetious	laborious	resonate
candid	facile	labyrinth	resurgence
cantankerous	facsimile	lackadaisical	reticent
capricious	fathom	lascivious	revoke
circumspect	gait	lateral	rife
complacent	generate	laud	ruse
deferential	hindrance	lax	satisfactory
denunciate	hodgepodge	legitimate	scrupulous
depravity	homogeneity	lenient	scurrilous
diaphanous	honorarium	levee	supercilious
disingenuous	hypocritical	licentious	supplant
dowager	hypothetical	lithe	tedious
dubious	idealize	loath	temperate
ebullient		loathe	unbridled
efface		malediction	unrelenting
			unwarranted

Answers

Puzzle #1
1. cacophonous
2. efface
3. ephemeral
4. imponderable
5. ire
6. lackadaisical
7. metaphorical
8. nautical
9. presumptuous
10. lenient

Bonus: capricious

Puzzle #2
1. levee
2. prohibitive
3. quintessence
4. impel
5. fabrication
6. explicit
7. tedious
8. loathe
9. erroneous
10. diaphanous

Bonus: licentious

Puzzle #3
1. depravity
2. facsimile
3. bask
4. disingenuous
5. lascivious

6. hindrance
7. malediction
8. facile
9. unrelenting
10. repudiate

Bonus: ambivalent

Puzzle #4
1. beckon
2. resonate
3. temperate
4. impetuous
5. idealize
6. hindrance
7. satisfactory
8. reticent
9. mantel
10. altruism

Bonus: complacent

Puzzle #5
1. anomalous
2. supercilious
3. ruse
4. epitome
5. juncture
6. laborious
7. laud
8. circumspect
9. erroneous
10. disingenuous

Bonus: scrupulous

Puzzle #6

1. bumptious
2. apprehensive
3. naive
4. idolize
5. homogeneity
6. supplant
7. migrant
8. idiosyncrasy
9. gait
10. blatant

Bonus: pedestrian

Puzzle #7

1. bolster
2. fathom
3. dowager
4. inept
5. hypothetical
6. facetious
7. effete
8. belligerence
9. unbridled
10. loath

Bonus: hodgepodge

Puzzle #8

1. unwarranted
2. mantel
3. generate
4. dubious
5. kimono

6. junction
7. insight
8. lascivious
9. scurrilous
10. lithe

Bonus: denunciate

Puzzle #9

1. lax
2. revoke
3. labyrinth
4. hypocritical
5. facile
6. rife
7. ebullient
8. lateral
9. effect
10. honorarium

Bonus: exhilarate

Puzzle #10

1. mantle
2. embark
3. cantankerous
4. auspicious
5. egalitarian
6. endorse
7. candid
8. deferential
9. ebullient
10. legitimate

Bonus: resurgence

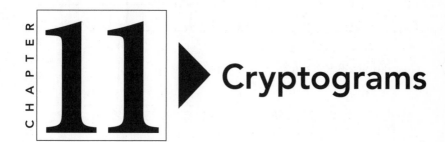

Cryptograms

In this chapter, you will learn the spellings and definitions of common PSAT/SAT vocabulary words through fun cryptograms.

Instructions

Fill in numbers 1 through 26 in order in the following hint boxes. You will then have a number corresponding to each letter for the entire alphabet.

Then, use these letter-number pairs to solve each definition . Once you've figured out the definition, unscramble each word.

Answers are found at the back of the chapter. Don't peek!

Cryptogram #1

G	D	P	S	Z	B	E	X	F	A	V	C	Y	H	M	U	L	T	Q	K	W	I	N	J	R	O

Unscramble: B E L L A I

$$\overline{17}\ \overline{7}\ \overline{1}\ \overline{10}\ \overline{17}\ \overline{17}\ \overline{18} \quad \overline{25}\ \overline{7}\ \overline{4}\ \overline{3}\ \overline{26}\ \overline{23}\ \overline{4}\ \overline{22}\ \overline{6}\ \overline{17}\ \overline{7}$$

$$\overline{26}\ \overline{6}\ \overline{17}\ \overline{22}\ \overline{1}\ \overline{10}\ \overline{18} \quad \overline{7}\ \overline{2}$$

Cryptogram #2

H	Z	A	T	N	F	R	B	C	Y	D	U	W	E	V	G	O	X	S	Q	I	K	P	M	J	L

Unscramble: R E D L A I D E

$$\overline{4}\ \overline{1}\ \overline{7}\ \overline{17}\ \overline{13}\ \overline{5} \quad \overline{17}\ \overline{6}\ \overline{6} \quad \overline{9}\ \overline{17}\ \overline{12}\ \overline{7}\ \overline{19}\ \overline{14}$$

Cryptogram #3

Y	R	O	Z	A	M	S	B	L	P	I	X	D	W	F	N	G	V	H	T	J	U	Q	K	E	C

Unscramble: V E Y L

$$\overline{11}\ \overline{6}\ \overline{10}\ \overline{3}\ \overline{7}\ \overline{25} \quad \overline{3}\ \overline{2} \quad \overline{26}\ \overline{3}\ \overline{9}\ \overline{9}\ \overline{25}\ \overline{26}\ \overline{20}$$

$$\overline{7}\ \overline{25}\ \overline{11}\ \overline{4}\ \overline{25}$$

Cryptogram #4

L	U	Z	C	H	Y	A	J	X	K	I	O	W	E	F	T	G	D	V	S	B	R	Q	N	M	P

Unscramble: F I D D I F T E N

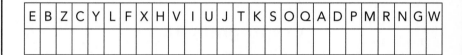

5 14 20 11 16 7 23 16   20 14 1 15   18 12 2 21 16 11 23 17

Cryptogram #5

E	B	Z	C	Y	L	F	X	H	V	I	U	J	T	K	S	O	Q	A	D	P	M	R	N	G	W

Unscramble: S A B E A

6 17 26 1 23   17 23   20 1 25 23 19 20 1

Cryptogram #6

M	E	Q	N	L	O	I	R	V	K	W	G	S	X	P	C	J	A	Y	D	F	U	B	T	Z	H

Unscramble: R E A T A L L

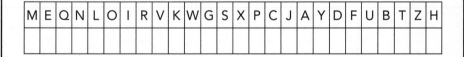

24 6   24 26 2   13 7 20 2

Cryptogram #7

V	G	J	S	E	B	O	I	Z	F	Y	H	W	K	N	R	P	U	T	L	A	M	Q	D	C	X

Unscramble: R A B Y A R R I T

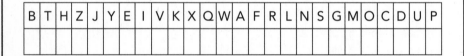

16 21 15 24 7 22   4 18 6 3 5 25 19   19 7

8 15 24 8 1 8 24 18 21 20   3 18 24 2 22 5 15 19

Cryptogram #8

B	T	H	Z	J	Y	E	I	V	K	X	Q	W	A	F	R	L	N	S	G	M	O	C	D	U	P

Unscramble: R E D E T

26 25 2   22 15 15   22 16   24 8 19 23 22 25 16 14 20 7

Cryptogram #9

G	Z	C	X	H	Q	I	W	S	J	A	O	D	F	E	R	B	N	T	M	K	V	L	P	U	Y

Unscramble: V O R A D A B

$$\overline{}\ \overline{}\ \overline{}\ \overline{}\ \overline{}\ \overline{}\ \overline{}\ \overline{} \quad \overline{}\ \overline{}\ \overline{}\ \overline{}\ \overline{}\ \overline{}\ \overline{}$$
11 16 16 12 1 11 18 19   13 7 9 24 23 11 26

$$\overline{}\ \overline{} \quad \overline{}\ \overline{}\ \overline{}\ \overline{}\ \overline{}\ \overline{}\ \overline{}\ \overline{}$$
12 14   17 12 23 13 18 15 9 9

Cryptogram #10

I	K	B	Z	G	X	D	E	Y	A	W	S	O	T	L	V	C	R	H	U	N	F	Q	P	J	M

Unscramble: P Y H A T A

$$\overline{}\ \overline{}\ \overline{}\ \overline{} \quad \overline{}\ \overline{} \quad \overline{}\ \overline{}\ \overline{}\ \overline{}\ \overline{}\ \overline{} \quad \overline{}\ \overline{}$$
15 10 17 2   13 22   8 21 8 18 5 9   13 18

$$\overline{}\ \overline{}\ \overline{}\ \overline{}\ \overline{}\ \overline{}\ \overline{}\ \overline{}$$
1 21 14 8 18 8 12 14

Answers

Cryptogram #1
legally responsible or obligated
LIABLE

Cryptogram #2
thrown off course
DERAILED

Cryptogram #3
Impose or collect; seize
LEVY

Cryptogram #4
hesitant; self-doubting
DIFFIDENT

Cryptogram #5
lower or degrade
ABASE

Cryptogram #6
to the side
LATERAL

Cryptogram #7
random; subject to individual judgment
ARBITRARY

Cryptogram #8
put off or discourage
DETER

Cryptogram #9
arrogant display of boldness
BRAVADO

Cryptogram #10
lack of energy or interest
APATHY

Set a Foolproof Strategy

12 ▶ Planning and Preparing

Congratulations! You've finished the games in this book—which means you've taken a big step in improving your vocabulary skills. However, you may still have some time before the big day, right? Let's look at some more preparation you can do, to make sure your score is the absolute best it can be.

Six Months Before Test Day

So, you've got some time before the PSAT or SAT exam. That's great! Read on for some additional things you can do to prepare yourself for the big day—from supersizing your vocabulary to learning the ins and outs of the exam and making sure you're in good shape—both physically and mentally—on the day of the test.

Keep Up the Vocab Workout

By now you're aware that a good working vocabulary is an important asset on the Verbal sections of the PSAT and SAT. But did you know that the best way to learn vocabulary is also the easiest? Simply keep an eye out for unfamiliar words, add them to a running list, and then set aside a few minutes each day to learn some of the words on that list.

DECONSTRUCT, DECONSTRUCT, DECONSTRUCT

When learning new words, remember to break them down into roots, prefixes, and suffixes (as you learned in Chapters 1 through 3). You'll be surprised to see how quickly knowing these will help you figure out definitions—and increase your vocabulary!

Let's figure it out. How much time do you have until you take the exam? Is it a month, three months, a year? Whatever the length of time, you still have a chance to substantially improve your vocabulary before sitting down with that test booklet.

So here's what you do. Count out the number of days before test day. (Don't count the night before—you'll be busy resting and rewarding yourself that night. See "The Night Before Test Day" in this chapter for more details.) Then, multiply the number of days by five. The result is the number of new vocabulary words you'll know before the exam—by learning just five words a day. You can handle that, right? Of course you can!

VOCAB IN A FLASH

One easy way to learn your five new words per day is to use flashcards. Write a word on one side and the definition on the other, then keep the cards with you to practice whenever you have spare time. You can use them to study alone, or quiz a friend—then have that friend quiz you. Flashcards are a great way to get in some study time anywhere. (If you're a techie or the kind of person who carries a mobile device at all times, check out some of the free flashcard apps available.)

Remember to be on the lookout for new words everywhere. Jot down unfamiliar words you see on signs, hear in conversations, or come across while reading your favorite magazines. Make sure your new words list is always with you, so you can keep track of the ones you've learned and the ones you have on deck for the next time you have some time to kill!

Familiarize Yourself with the Exam

One big advantage you can give yourself on the day of the test is to know exactly what to expect, from how the exam is structured to approximately how long it will take you to complete each section and when to spend time figuring out an answer versus when to just make an educated guess. Fortunately, there are lots of practice tools out there that can help you do just that.

TALK IT OUT

When you learn a new word, try to use it as soon as you can. Practical knowledge—using something you've learned in the real world—is often the best way to really integrate something into your mind. So talk to your friends, your family, and your teachers using SAT words—to help you remember those words when it counts. Work these words into e-mails and essays. See how many people can keep up with your vocab skills!

Books

You can find the most up-to-date practice books in your local library or in most bookstores. If you decide to use books to take practice exams, it's especially important to make sure that you're giving yourself the same amount of time to complete each section as you'll get on the day of the test. You can find some suggestions for good books in the Resources section on page 151.

Online

Another great way to practice for the PSAT or SAT exam is to take an actual practice exam online. These exams often consist of actual questions used on past SAT exams. There are lots of practice tests available on the Internet—some are free, and others can be accessed for a fee—but a great place to start is the College Board website, www.colleg-eboard.com. Some other suggestions for good practice sites are located in the Resources section on page 151.

Time Management

While you're taking practice tests, be sure to keep an eye on the time. The basic rule of PSAT/SAT test taking is to allow yourself one minute per question, but depending on your strengths, some questions will take you less time, and others will take more. Don't consider the "one-minute rule" to be hard and fast, but do be aware of the amount of time you're taking—and don't spend too much time on any one question.

When working on a question you're not sure of, be sure to eliminate wrong answer choices wherever you can. Cross out the ones you know are wrong on the test sheet so you can concentrate on the remaining possibilities, giving yourself a better chance at finding the right answer.

And don't forget that you can always go back and revisit questions if you come to the end of a section before time is up. Just circle the number of the question so you can find it easily if you have extra time at the end to go back to it.

Don't Rely on Guessing

The SAT has been set up to penalize test-takers for random guessing. So making an educated guess if you think you know the answer is fine, but don't just fill in answers as time runs out just to answer questions. You'll lose more for an incorrect guess than you will if you just leave that question blank.

Play to Your Strengths

You know better than anyone else what comes easily for you, and what you have to work hard on. So if one type of question in a particular section is easier for you than another, skip right to it and answer those questions first. Remember, you get the same point value for an easy correct answer as you do for a difficult one—so answer the easy questions first and save the ones you find harder for last!

A Few Weeks Before Test Day

As test day looms closer, you may start to feel a bit of panic set in. Don't worry, that's normal. Besides, you have nothing to worry about because you've been preparing all along. So take a deep breath and relax!

Schedule Study Time

One way to really set your mind at ease is to put together a study schedule for the next few weeks leading up to the exam. Try to map out a half hour to an hour a day, and decide what you'll be working on in advance. Then, when you've completed your study session, stop! Studying regularly in small intervals is often more effective than trying to cram too much information into long, sleepless nights. When your allotted study time is up, close your book, turn off the computer, and go do something fun.

Step Away from the Chips!

You've probably heard that the best way to prepare yourself for anything stressful is to be sure that you're in good health. Lots of us tend to reach for the snacks while studying—and even more so when feeling stressed out over a big exam—but it goes without saying that healthy foods are best for keeping your mind and body in tip-top shape.

And speaking of shape, you know what else is a great stress-buster? Exercise. See Chapter 13 for more details, but the fact is that regular exercise helps keep the mind alert, reduces fatigue, and results in a better night's sleep.

A Few Days Before Test Day

A few days before the exam is the best time for some last-minute brush-ups. Grab your book or log on to your computer and take a practice exam one final time. Focus on your problem areas, and give yourself a little extra study time in those areas. Review everything you know about the SAT exam to make sure that there will be absolutely no surprises on test day.

Do a Dry Run

It's not only a good idea to be as familiar as you can be with the test itself, but it's also smart to know exactly where you'll be going—and how you'll be getting there—on the day of the test so you don't wake up in a panic about it. Find out where your test center is located, and go there at the same time and day of the week as your exam is scheduled. Take the same mode of transportation you will be using on exam day, so you can get a good sense ahead of time about unexplained glitches in Google Maps, construction that may force you to take a detour, or unforeseen public transportation issues.

Review Test-Taking Policies

There are very specific guidelines that determine what you can and can't bring into the test center, as well as security and fairness regulations in place at the test centers. Be sure to get a copy of these guidelines (either from your guidance office at school or online at The College Board website) and familiarize yourself with them, so you know what you can expect when you arrive.

Get Organized

Gather together everything you will need the day of the test and put it in a safe place (see Chapter 14 for a checklist of essential items). That way, you won't have to worry about rushing around before you leave in the morning, looking for your admission ticket or a calculator.

The Day Before Test Day

You've worked hard, and your efforts are about to pay off. But it's the day before the exam, and you're going to work really hard tomorrow to do the best you can on the PSAT or SAT. You're as ready as you'll ever be, so take this opportunity to give yourself a well-deserved break.

Tonight, your assignment is to watch a good movie, spend some time with your friends, play a video game or board game with family members, or do another fun and relaxing activity. Be sure to get to bed early enough to guarantee a full night's rest. The only thing you should not do is think about the SAT exam.

On the Big Day

It's finally here! The day you've been preparing for all these weeks and months has arrived, but don't worry. You've studied, you've learned how the test is administered and what to look for, and you know exactly how long it's going to take to get to the test center. So you have nothing at all to worry about. Just concentrate on doing your best on the exam.

Prepare with Protein

You've got a long day ahead of you, so be sure to start the morning right. Eat a good breakfast, which ideally should be rich in protein. (It's widely believed that protein helps increase alertness and response time.) Some good choices are eggs, grains, nuts, or dairy products such as yogurt or cottage cheese. Whatever you choose, make sure to eat enough. You don't want everyone to hear your stomach growling half an hour into the exam.

Load Up on Layers

You won't have any control over the temperature in the room in which you'll be sitting for the next several hours, and the last thing you need is to be distracted by chattering teeth or sweat pooling across your forehead. Wear something comfortable, but be sure to include layers, so you're guaranteed not to be too hot or too warm while you're taking the test.

Keep an Eye on the Clock

Make sure that you give yourself plenty of time to get to the test center, even if major traffic or a natural disaster suddenly decides to get in your way. You don't want to be rushing into the room at the last minute.

That's it! You're ready to go out there and get a great score on the PSAT or SAT. Just one final thing—make sure you have a post-test celebration in mind, because you definitely deserve it.

Good luck!

13 ▶ Anxiety-Busting Exercises

Let's face it. As well prepared as you are for your test, you might be feeling some stress and anxiety about it. This is normal—anxiety is a common response to difficult situations, and it happens to many people.

Luckily, though, there are many things you can do to combat stress and anxiety, and ensure that you arrive at the test center relaxed and ready to take on the exam. The first thing to do is remind yourself that you've studied and practiced, so you're undeniably ready for the challenge. Feel confident in the knowledge that, unlike many others, you're walking into that exam room prepared for what lies ahead.

But sometimes knowing that you're ready isn't enough. In that case, there are some simple exercises you can do to keep yourself calm and collected. These exercises can help you deal with stress, and can be done anywhere, anytime. Whenever you feel yourself starting to panic about the upcoming exam, just take some time to do one of the following.

Deep Breathing

Just breathe in and out? Really? Yes, it's that simple. Take a few minutes to sit back, close your eyes, and concentrate on taking deep, regular breaths. This simple act will help slow your heart rate and make you feel calmer.

Muscle Relaxation

Sit in a chair or on the floor, or lie on your bed. Begin by tensing each of your muscles for a count of ten, then slowly relaxing them. Work from your toes up to your shoulders, and then back down again. You'll feel more rested and relaxed in no time.

Visualization

It may sound silly, but many people believe that they do better in stressful situations and accomplish goals more easily if they've first pictured themselves succeeding. So, take a few minutes to sit back, relax, and imagine yourself walking into the test center. You've prepared, you've got all your materials with you, you've slept well and eaten a good breakfast, and you're armed with the knowledge you need to ace the test. Now, picture yourself leaning over the test booklet, flipping confidently through it, knowing some answers right away, making educated guesses about others, and knowing that it's okay to leave some blank if you really have no idea. Then picture yourself confidently closing the booklet, standing up, and heading out to celebrate when you're done. It doesn't seem so bad now, does it?

Meditation

The idea behind meditation is to relax your body while concentrating on one thing. Sit or lie in a comfortable position, close your eyes, and try thinking about a positive outcome on the exam. Breathe deeply in and out for ten minutes. You'll find that you feel more relaxed and refreshed afterward.

If you're familiar with the moves, yoga is also a great way to relax your body and prepare your mind to concentrate. But don't strain your muscles doing anything you're not used to—the point here is to relax, not to put undue stress on your body.

Exercise

Exercise is another great way to get rid of stress. But exercise doesn't have to consist of lifting weights or running on the treadmill at the gym; it can be a game of touch football with your friends, playing with your dog in the park, or even some time spent dancing to your favorite songs in your room. Work up a sweat and put those anxious thoughts out of your mind. Your body—and your brain—will thank you for it!

Walk Away from Naysayers

Sometimes it helps to vent about a stressful situation to family or friends, but other times it can add to your anxiety. If someone you know is constantly complaining about how hard the SAT exam is, or how she knows she's going to crash and burn, it's okay to change the subject. Really. Just shrug and say that all you can do is prepare, and then go do exactly that.

Regardless of what method you choose, the important thing to remember is to not let anxiety put you on edge before the exam. Keep in mind that the hardest part of taking the PSAT or SAT is often the time leading up to the exam itself. Just do the best you can, and don't worry about anything else.

CHAPTER

Test-Day Checklist

What to Bring

- ☐ photo ID
- ☐ admission ticket
- ☐ sharpened pencils (Number 2)
- ☐ eraser
- ☐ calculator (graphing, scientific, or four-function ONLY) with extra batteries
- ☐ water
- ☐ snack
- ☐ watch (with no audio alerts)

What NOT to Bring

- ☐ mobile phone
- ☐ iPod, MP3 player, or CD player
- ☐ iPad or laptop computer
- ☐ Blackberry, mobile organizer, or PDA
- ☐ highlighters, markers, pens, or colored pencils
- ☐ notes or other paper

- ☐ books
- ☐ camera or photographic equipment

What to Do

- ☐ eat a good breakfast
- ☐ dress in layers so you're comfortable in the exam room
- ☐ pack some water and a healthy snack for your break
- ☐ leave early so you are sure to arrive on time, even if there's traffic

Glossary ▶

A

abase lower or degrade

abashed ashamed

abdicate give up a position of leadership

abridge shorten or edit down while keeping the essential elements

accolade praise

achromatic without hue; free from color

acumen keen insight and perception

adroit skillful

adversary opponent

adverse contrary or opposed; unfavorable

advocate argue in favor of something

aesthetic appreciation of beauty or art

affinity relationship or close connection

affluent wealthy, rich

agriculture science or practice of farming

allege to insist or assert, usually without proof

allusion indirect reference

altruism unselfish concern for others; self-sacrifice

ambivalent undecided; unclear

amoral neither moral nor immoral; being beyond a particular code of conduct

amorous showing love

anachronism an artifact that belongs to another time

analogy comparison

anecdote short story or account of something interesting

annihilate vanquish completely; make someone or something cease to exist

anomalous odd; not fitting a particular pattern

anthology collection of writings

antiseptic sterile; thoroughly clean and free of disease

apathy lack of energy or interest

apparition something that "appears"; a ghost

appraise set a value or estimate the cost of something

apprehensive suspicious; fearful

apprise give notice; tell

arable capable of growing crops

arbitrary random; subject to individual judgment

arbitration resolution of a dispute by an impartial party

arboreal of or relating to trees

arcane obscure; requiring secret or mysterious knowledge

archaic old-fashioned; outdated

arduous difficult

arid extremely dry; lacking sufficient rainfall

articulate express well in words

artifact something created by humans and remaining from a particular era

artisan craftsperson

ascetic practicing extreme self-denial

aspersion negative or disparaging remark

assuage lessen; make better

atrophy wither away, decay

auger tool used for making holes or removing loose material

augur a person who foretells events or sees the future

auspicious favorable; fortunate

averse having a feeling of intense dislike or repulsion

axiom statement that is widely accepted as true

azure light shade of blue

B

ballad narrative poem, often in lyric form

banal dull, unoriginal

bask lie or relax in a warm environment; take pleasure or enjoyment

bauble trinket

beckon summon or signal with an inviting wave or nod

bedlam madhouse; scene of uproar and confusion

belie misrepresent or give a false impression

bellicose warlike

belligerence aggression

benefactor person who gives charitable gifts

benevolent kind

benign mild or gentle

beseech implore or beg

bestial animal-like

betroth promise to marry

bibliomania passion for books

bibulous fond of drinking alcoholic beverages

bide wait for

bifurcate cut in two

bilateral two-sided

bilingual speaking two languages

blanch whiten; turn pale

blasé sophisticated; unconcerned with pleasure or excitement

blatant obvious

bleak hopeless; barren and lacking in warmth or life

blithe joyous

boll round pod or seed capsule

bolster support

bombastic too elaborate; exaggerated

boor one who is rude or crude

botanical of or related to plants

braggart someone who boasts or brags

bravado arrogant display of boldness

brevity shortness; conciseness

brigand someone who lives by plundering or theft

brine strong saline or salt water

browbeat intimidate with strong language

brusque blunt or rude in manner or speech

bucolic of or related to the countryside and farming

bullock young ox or steer

bumptious aggressively conceited and presumptuous

C

cacophonous noisy; unpleasant sounding

callous cruel; unfeeling

candid truthful or sincere; free from bias

cantankerous ill-tempered; cranky

canvas tightly woven material used for tents and sails; framed cloth for painting

canvass examine or inspect; seek orders or votes

capricious fickle; changing on a whim

censor person who supervises conduct or morals; suppress or delete anything

censure official reprimand or condemnation

cerebral brainy; intelligent

cherished cared for; loved

chicanery trickery

chide scold

chronicle a written history; to write a history

churlish ill-mannered; rude

circumlocution ambiguous, indirect, and wordy language

circumspect careful to consider all feelings and consequences; prudent

cite refer to or quote authoritatively; call upon officially

clairvoyant able to perceive things (such as the future) that the normal senses cannot

cliché overused expression

cohesive forming a whole; sticking together

collateral property pledged as security for a debt; accompanying; secondary

comely pleasing; attractive

compare find similarities or resemblances

complacent smug; self-satisfied

complement make something complete

compliment expression of respect or affection; good wishes

compose form; produce; create

comprise made up of; included within a particular scope

concur agree

concurrent occurring at the same time; running parallel

conducive promoting or leading to something

conjugal of or relating to marriage; matrimonial

connote associate as a consequence; express indirectly or imply

connubial of or related to the relationship between spouses

conscience moral sense of right and wrong

conscious awake; aware

consecutive following one after the other in order

continual recurring in rapid succession; occurring frequently or regularly

continuous nonstop; continuing uninterrupted

contrast find a degree of difference

convince encourage; talk someone into something

convivial friendly; sociable

convoluted complicated; long-winded

cosmopolitan sophisticated; worldly

council an advisory or legislative body or group

counsel advice, policy, or plan of action

counterfeit fake

credence belief

cryptic hidden; mysterious

cultivate nurture; prepare and improve

curtail lessen or reduce

D

decent appropriate; free from immodesty or obscenity

decimate destroy or reduce drastically

decipher decode; interpret

decorous proper; correct

deferential showing esteem or respect

deft skillful

defuse make less harmful or tense

denote indicate; make known

denunciate speak out against someone or something

depravity moral corruption

derailed thrown off course

derivative unoriginal

descent downward inclination; deriving from an ancestor

desolate dreary; barren

despotic acting like a tyrant

destitute completely impoverished

deter put off or discourage

detritus trash

diaphanous thin; transparent

dichotomy division into two contradictory groups

dictum often-used saying

didactic intended to teach or instruct

diffident hesitant; self-doubting

diffuse not concentrated; spread out

digress go off-subject; turn attention away

dilettante someone who dabbles in the arts

dirge somber, mournful song for the dead

discreet modest; having good moral judgment

discrete separate; individually distinct

disdain contempt

disingenuous false; calculating

disinterested impartial; unbiased

dispassionate unbiased; fair

dispute argue or debate; oppose; verbal disagreement or controversy

distend swell out

docile easily taught or managed

dowager wealthy elderly woman

dubious doubtful

E

ebullient showing enthusiasm or exhilaration

eccentric peculiar; odd

ecstatic overwhelmingly happy

edict formal or authoritative statement or announcement

efface eliminate; obliterate

effect result brought about by something else

effervescent lively; bubbly

effete weak; no longer strong or vital

effusive excessively emotional; "gushing"

egalitarian equal; believer in equality

egregious conspicuously bad

egress place of exit

elated thrilled; overjoyed

elegy lyric poem lamenting the dead

elicit to draw out (especially in reference to emotion or information)

elite privileged

elocution correct and proper inflection and intonation in speech

elude avoid or escape

emaciate waste away; cause to lose flesh

emanate come out or flow forth from a source

emancipate free from the power or control of others; release from bondage

embark make a start; go on board

embellish make beautiful or elegant with ornamentation

embezzle steal money by falsifying documents

emigrant one who departs a country to settle elsewhere

eminent standing out or above in quality or position

empathy sharing another's emotions or feelings

enamor fill with love for someone or something

endorse sign; support

enigma puzzle; riddle

ensure to make certain

ephemeral short-lived

epistolary of or relating to letters and letter-writing

epitome a typical example

equitable fair and equal

equivocate ambiguous or vague in speech; noncommittal

erroneous wrong

erudite showing vast knowledge; learned

esoteric limited to a small circle; requiring specialized information

evasive avoiding or hiding something

exhilarate excite

explicit very clear and direct

F

fabrication something made up; lie; untruth

facetious meant to be humorous or not taken seriously

facile easily accomplished or attained

facsimile exact copy or reproduction

fallible capable of making an error or mistake

famish suffer from extreme hunger; starve

fathom unit that measures water depth; penetrate; understand; probe

fecund fertile; fruitful

feral wild; untamed

fervent hot; passionate

fidelity loyalty; devotion

figuratively symbolically; metaphorically

filial referring to the child-parent relationship

flaunt show off shamelessly

florid excessively elaborate or showy; flowery

flotsam floating wreckage or rubbish

flounder struggle or thrash about

flout disregard; show scorn or contempt

foraging searching for food

foreboding prediction, omen, or sense of doom

foreword introductory note or preface

forward toward the front; send on or pass along

founder one who founds or establishes; give way or sink

frugal economical

funereal of or relating to a burial or grave

G

gait manner of walking or moving

gambol frolic; skip about

gamut entire series or range

garnish decorate or accessorize

garrote strangulation

gendarme police officer or soldier, especially in France

generate cause or bring into existence

genteel having an elegant or superior quality

germane relevant and appropriate

gesticulate make movements or gestures while speaking

ghastly horrible or terrifying

gibe tease; taunt

glutinous glue-like; gummy

gluttonous having an enormous appetite

gourmand one who greatly enjoys eating and drinking

grandiose exaggerated or overblown

H

habitable suitable for living

hackneyed overused; trite

halcyon calm and peaceful; tranquil

harangue give a ranting speech

hardy able to withstand adverse conditions

heinous extremely wicked; reprehensible

herbivorous feeding only on plants

hereditary occurring among members of a family

hindrance something that interferes with or delays action or progress

hirsute coarsely hairy; shaggy

hodgepodge odd mixture or combination

homage respect; honor

homogeneity being similar or comparable in nature

honorarium compensation for a professional service

hypocritical deceptive; pretending to be good or virtuous

hypothetical based on guesswork; not proven

I

iconoclast someone who goes against accepted authority

idealize regard someone or something as perfect

idiom phrase that cannot be translated literally into another language

idiosyncrasy quirk or unique trait

idolize worship or adore unquestionably and to excess

ignominious state of dishonor or shame

illicit unlawful

illusion something that is misleading or deceptive

imbibe absorb; drink

imbroglio complicated situation; entanglement

immigrant someone who settles in a new country

imminent at hand; about to occur

immoral unethical; morally objectionable

impeccable faultless; without errors or flaws

impecunious habitually lacking money; poor

impede get in the way; hinder

impel urge or force to action

impervious unaffected; impenetrable

impetuous impulsive

imply suggest; express or state indirectly

imponderable impossible to understand

incidence frequency of occurrence

incidents happenings; events that could lead to a grave consequence

incite move to action; stir up

indigence extreme poverty

indigenous occurring naturally or originating in a particular region

inept clumsy or inexpert

infatuated foolishly or extravagantly in love

infer guess; deduce

inflammable able to be set on fire

ingenious resourceful, clever

inherent inbuilt; genetic

inoculate introduce a microorganism in order to treat or prevent a disease; vaccinate

insight penetration; seeing the inner nature of something

insure provide or obtain insurance; take precaution

intricate complicated

iota shred; tiny amount

ire great anger; wrath

iridescent showing varying rainbow colors

irrefutable cannot be proved wrong

irrelevant having no connection with an issue or subject; unrelated

irreverent showing disrespect

J

jargon slang

jeopardize put into danger; threaten

jibe agree or be in accord; shift suddenly and forcibly

jocular humorous

jovial jolly; full of good humor

jubilant extremely joyful

judicious fair and equal; having good judgment or common sense

junction place where two or more things come together; being joined

juncture event that occurs at a critical time

jurisprudence philosophy, science, and study of law

juxtapose place side by side for contrasting effect

K

kiln furnace or oven for drying or hardening pottery or bricks

kimono loose robe

kinship relationship or affinity between people

knave one who is tricky or dishonest

L

laborious requiring much physical effort

labyrinth maze; complex system of paths or tunnels

lacerate cut, tear, or rip irregularly

lackadaisical dreamy; without interest or enthusiasm

laconic brief or terse in writing or speech

lament express regret

languid lacking in liveliness or spirit; dreamy

lascivious driven by lust; lewd

latent existing or present, but concealed or inactive

lateral to the side

laud praise, glorify, or honor

lax lacking in strength or firmness

legible capable of being read or deciphered

legitimate lawful or valid

lenient not strict; permissive

lethargic fatigue; abnormal drowsiness or weariness

levee embankment or pier; formal reception of guests

leviathan largest or most massive of its kind

levity humor

levy impose or collect; seize

lexicon vocabulary

liable legally responsible or obligated

libel written statement that is false and malicious

licentious lacking moral discipline or restraint; lewd

linear of or along or relating to a line

literally actually; word-for-word

lithe moving or bending with ease

litigious eager or prone to engaging in lawsuits

livid red in color; furious

loath unwilling; reluctant

loathe great dislike or disgust

loquacious talkative

lucrative profitable

luminary prominent or brilliant person body that gives light

luminous glowing brightly; radiant

M

magnanimous noble; generous in spirit

maize corn

malediction evil speech; curse

maleficent harmful or evil

malevolent wishing harm to others

malign make defamatory or contemptuous statements; "badmouth"

malleable easily influenced; changeable

mandate official command or instruction

maneuver tactic; deliberate, coordinated movement

manifesto statement of values

mantel shelf set above a fireplace

mantle cloak or cape as a symbol of authority

marital of or relating to marriage

martial suited for war; related to military life

mediocre average

mendicancy begging

mercenary someone who would do anything for money

metaphorical figurative; not literal

migrant someone who travels from one region to another in search of work

milieu environment; surroundings

miscreant someone who has behaved badly or illegally

mitigated made less severe

munificent generosity; giving or bestowing liberally

N

naïve unsophisticated; inexperienced

narrate tell a story

nascent just begun; in early stages of development

natal of or related to birth

nautical of or related to ships, navigation, or sailing

necropolis city of the dead

nefarious extremely wicked

neophyte beginner

nocturnal of or related to the night

noisome offensive, especially to the sense of smell

nonchalant not caring; indifferent

nonflammable unable to be set on fire

nostalgia longing for the past

notable worthy of notice; especially

noticeable able to be perceived or detected

noxious harmful or destructive

O

oblique slanting; not straightforward

obliterate wipe out

obsolete no longer practiced, used, or accepted

obtrusive undesirably prominent; easily seen

ocular of or related to the eye

odious hateful

official v. relating to an office or position; n. one who holds such a position

officious kind; dutiful

olfactory of or related to the sense of smell

ominous foreshadowing evil; foreboding

onus burden or responsibility

opulent superior in quality; rich

orthographical concerned with writing and spelling

oscillate swing or move back and forth

osculate kiss

ossified become fixed or rigid

ostentatious showy; conspicuous

oust push out of a position of authority

P

pacifist someone who opposes war

palette range or particular use of color; flat tray to hold paint

palliate make better; lessen the seriousness

pallid pale; lacking color

palpable can be felt

panacea remedy for all diseases and ills; a "cure-all"

paradox contradictory statement or group of statements

paragon model or example of perfection

paramour unlawful or illicit lover

parsimony stinginess

pedestrian someone on foot, walking; unimaginative or boring

penultimate next-to-last

penurious miserly

perfidy treachery; betrayal

perspicacious acutely insightful and wise

perspicuous transparent; clear and precise

persuade plead with; urge

peruse read carefully

pittance very small sum

placid serene; undisturbed

precede be, go, or come ahead or in front of; surpass

prescribe recommend; specify with authority

presumptuous assuming too much

primeval ancient; original

principal educator in a position of executive authority; original amount of a debt

principle basic truth or belief; rule of personal conduct

privation extreme poverty; lack of essential necessities

proceed continue; follow a certain course

profligacy wasteful and extravagant behavior

prohibitive very expensive

proscribe condemn or forbid as harmful

proximity closeness

prudence wise discretion and sound judgment

pugnacious aggressive and combative

purvey to supply or sell

Q

qualm feeling of unease

quandary confusing predicament; perplexity

queue line of people waiting in order of arrival

quibble trivial or unimportant argument or objection

quintessence most essential part

quixotic foolishly and impractically romantic

R

radiant bright, beaming

rapport harmony; mutual understanding

reconcile come to terms; bring back together; make compatible

repose rest; lie down

remedial meant to correct issues or gaps in students' basic knowledge

repudiate refuse to accept

resonate echo

respite a rest or break

resplendent glowing

resurgence revival

reticent reserved; restrained; reluctant to talk or draw attention

revoke take back

ribald crudely or coarsely humorous

rife abundant

ruddy having a reddish color

ruminate contemplate; reflect on or remember something

ruse trick

S

sagacious wise; shrewd

salient prominent; standing or projecting outward

salutary beneficial

sanguinary bloody; gory

sapient possessing great wisdom

satiate satisfy an appetite or desire

satisfactory adequate; sufficient

scintilla faint trace or spark

scrupulous doing only what is right or proper; having moral integrity

scrutinize examine closely

scurrilous using indecent or vulgar language; obscene

site location, scene, or point of occurrence

sparse thin, not thick

stationary fixed; unmoving

stationery writing materials; notepaper

stature height; quality or status gained by development

statute law or legislative act

stimulate rouse; excite to activity

stingy not generous; unwilling to spend

stringent strict

succumb to give in to or fall under the influence of something

supercilious arrogant or haughty

superfluous more than what is necessary or sufficient

supplant take the place of; serve as a substitute for

suppress put down or keep secret

surreptitiously stealthily or secretly

swarthy dark-colored or -complexioned

sympathy feeling of loyalty or support for another

T

tacit understood; expressed without words

taciturn quiet; not inclined to speak

tantamount equivalent in value, effect, or significance

tedious dull; boring

temperate mild; moderate

tenacity strength; firmness

terrestrial of or relating to earth or land

tirade long, angry speech

tome large book

torrid passionate; giving off intense heat

tortuous twisting and turning; devious or indirect tactics

torturous unpleasant or painful

tractable easily controlled

tranquil peaceful or calm

transcend to go beyond a certain limit; surpass

transgress go over a limit; violate

transient briefly passing through

travesty parody or poor imitation

tremulous fearful

trite unoriginal

truculent harsh; aggressively ferocious

turpitude depravity

U

ubiquitous present everywhere

ultimate most remote; last; best or most extreme

unbridled without restraint

understated unpretentious; restrained and in good taste

uninterested indifferent; not interested

universal occurring everywhere; including or covering everyone

unrelenting never giving up

unwarranted unjustified

usurp seize by force

utopia imaginary place of perfection

V

varied diverse; different kinds or sorts

variegated multicolored

venal capable of being bought; corrupt through bribery

venerable honored; worthy of respect

venial minor; pardonable

verbose wordy

verdant green in color

vestige trace of something lost or gone

viable workable; able to grow

virtuoso person who excels in an art (especially music)

visceral deep or instinctive; relating to the "guts"

vociferous blatant; conspicuous and offensive outcry

voracious excessively greedy or eager; large appetite or craving

W

wane decrease in size; dwindle

wanton lewd or lustful

wary careful; watchful

wily sly or crafty

winsome charming

wistful full of yearning and sadness

wrath vengeful anger

Y

yearling young animal between one and two years of age

yoke join or link

Z

zealot fanatical person

zeitgeist cultural, intellectual or moral tendencies of an era

zenith culminating or highest point

zephyr soft, gentle wind

Resources ▶

To further improve your vocabulary for the PSAT and SAT exams, be sure to check out these great resources, both in print and online.

Books

411 SAT Critical Reading Questions by LearningExpress (192 pages, LearningExpress, March 2007)

411 SAT Essay Prompts and Writing Questions by LearningExpress (192 pages, LearningExpress, August 2006).

500 Key Words for the SAT and How to Remember Them Forever! by Charles Gulotta and Trish Dardine (120 pages, Mostly Bright Ideas, August 2007).

The Official SAT Study Guide, 2nd Edition by The College Board (997 pages, College Board, July 2009).

SAT Score-Raising Dictionary by Kaplan (352 pages, Kaplan, May 2009).

SAT Success in 6 Simple Steps! by LearningExpress (224 pages, LearningExpress, February 2003).

SAT Vocabulary Prep Level 1 by Kaplan (352 pages, Kaplan, August 2008).

Up Your Score: The Underground Guide to the SAT by Larry Berger, Michael Colton, Manek Mistry, and Paul Rossi (328 pages, Workman, July 2008).

Online

Test Prep Review's PSAT Online Course
(www.testprepreview.com/psat_practice.htm)
TestPrepReview.com offers a free online course that will walk you through preparing for the PSAT.

College Board SAT Online Course
(https://satonlinecourse.collegeboard.com/SR/login/splashSchoolLogin.jsp)
The official source of the SAT, the College Board offers free official SAT practice tests on their website.

SparkNotes Vocabulary Builder
(www.sparknotes.com/testprep/books/newsat/powertactics/vocab/chapter2section2.rhtml)
SparkNotes analyzed the frequency with which certain words were used on the SAT over an eight-year span, and put together this free online vocabulary builder using those words. This is a great resource for building flashcards or other study guides for the SAT.

MajorTests.com SAT Word Lists
(www.majortests.com/sat/wordlist.php)
MajorTests.com has compiled an extensive collection of word lists that showcase the ones that are commonly used on the SAT. Use these lists to study by yourself, create flashcards, or test your friends.

FreeVocabulary.com's SuperVocab SAT Word List
(http://supervocab.com/satlist.cgi)
This list, featuring definitions from Merriam-Webster's online dictionary, allows you to test yourself by showing only the words—you have to click on each one for the definition.

NOTES

NOTES

NOTES

NOTES

NOTES

NOTES

NOTES